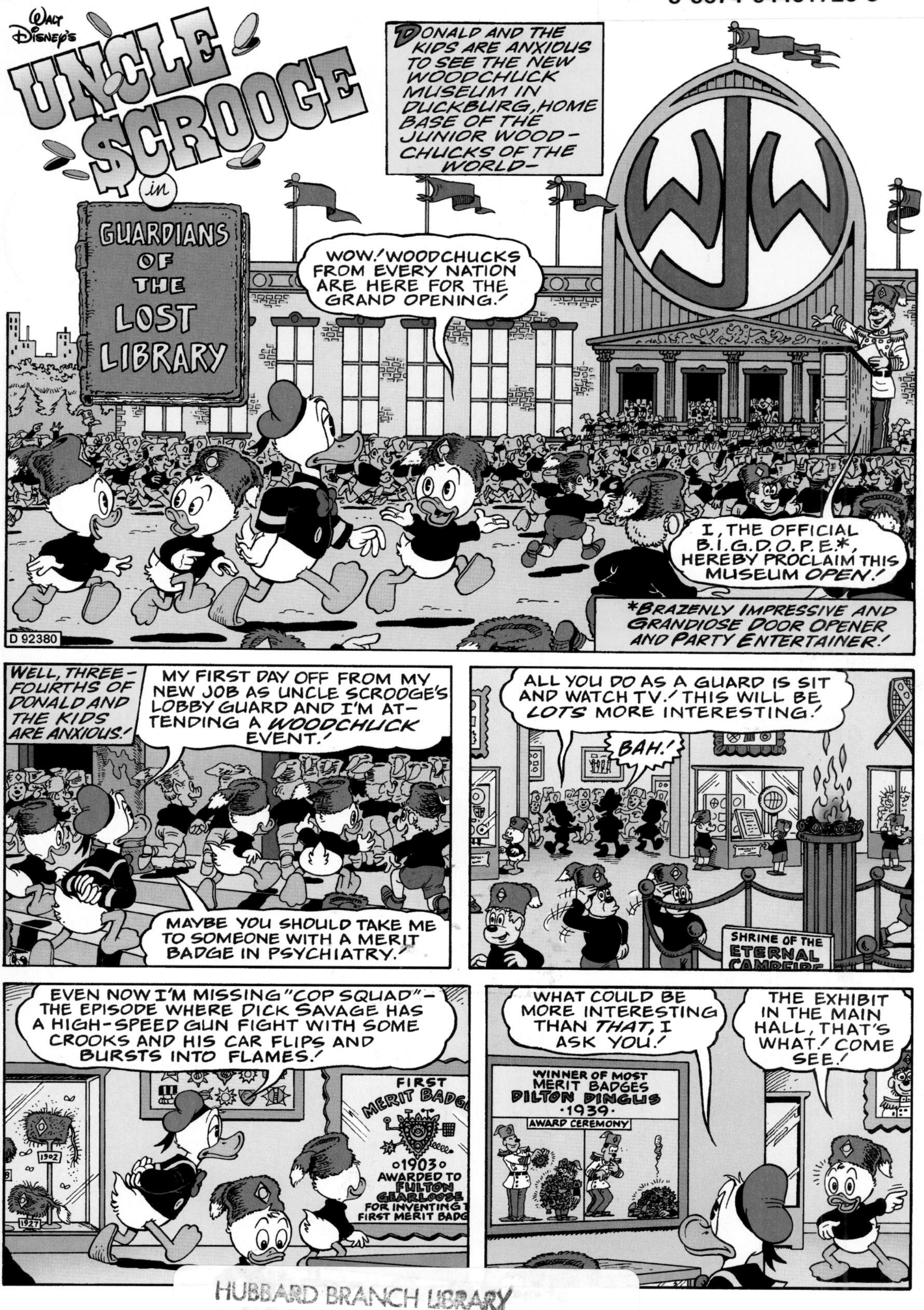
WALT DISNEY'S
UNCLE $CROOGE
in
GUARDIANS OF THE LOST LIBRARY
DONALD AND THE KIDS ARE ANXIOUS TO SEE THE NEW WOODCHUCK MUSEUM IN DUCKBURG, HOME BASE OF THE JUNIOR WOODCHUCKS OF THE WORLD—
WOW! WOODCHUCKS FROM EVERY NATION ARE HERE FOR THE GRAND OPENING!
I, THE OFFICIAL B.I.G.D.O.P.E.*, HEREBY PROCLAIM THIS MUSEUM OPEN!
*BRAZENLY IMPRESSIVE AND GRANDIOSE DOOR OPENER AND PARTY ENTERTAINER!
D 92380
WELL, THREE-FOURTHS OF DONALD AND THE KIDS ARE ANXIOUS!
MY FIRST DAY OFF FROM MY NEW JOB AS UNCLE SCROOGE'S LOBBY GUARD AND I'M ATTENDING A WOODCHUCK EVENT!
MAYBE YOU SHOULD TAKE ME TO SOMEONE WITH A MERIT BADGE IN PSYCHIATRY!
ALL YOU DO AS A GUARD IS SIT AND WATCH TV! THIS WILL BE LOTS MORE INTERESTING!
BAH!
SHRINE OF THE ETERNAL
EVEN NOW I'M MISSING "COP SQUAD"— THE EPISODE WHERE DICK SAVAGE HAS A HIGH-SPEED GUN FIGHT WITH SOME CROOKS AND HIS CAR FLIPS AND BURSTS INTO FLAMES!
1902
1927
FIRST MERIT BADGE
·1903·
AWARDED TO FULTON GEARLOOSE
FOR INVENTING FIRST MERIT BADGE
WHAT COULD BE MORE INTERESTING THAN THAT, I ASK YOU!
WINNER OF MOST MERIT BADGES
DILTON DINGUS
·1939·
AWARD CEREMONY
THE EXHIBIT IN THE MAIN HALL, THAT'S WHAT! COME SEE!

IT'S THE CENTERPIECE OF THE MUSEUM—THE OLDEST KNOWN COPY OF THE *JUNIOR WOODCHUCK GUIDEBOOK!*

IT ONCE BELONGED TO CLINTON COOT, SON OF THE FOUNDER OF DUCKBURG!

BRUH-THER! OLD-TIME WOODCHUCKS MUST HAVE EARNED MERIT BADGES IN COMPRESSED VERTEBRAE FOR CARRYING *THAT* BOOK IN THEIR BACKPACKS!

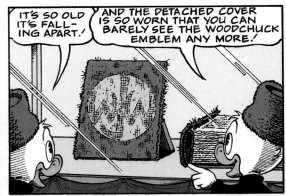

IT'S SO OLD IT'S FALL-ING APART!

AND THE DETACHED COVER IS SO WORN THAT YOU CAN BARELY SEE THE WOODCHUCK EMBLEM ANY MORE!

WOW! IT'S THE OLDEST COMPENDIUM OF ALL THAT WOODCHUCKS HOLD DEAR— UNSELFISH GOOD DEEDS, PROTECTION OF THE ENVIRONMENT, AND OUR *HIGHEST* IDEAL...

OBNOXIOUS KNOW-IT-ALLERY?

NO! THE *PRESERVATION OF KNOWLEDGE!* THAT'S THE BASIC PHILOSOPHY BEHIND THE JUNIOR WOODCHUCK GUIDEBOOK! WE...

OFFICIAL MUSEUM *A.N.S.W.E.R. MAN*

OUT! OUT!

AWESOMELY NOTEWORTHY SENIOR WOODCHUCK, EXPERT RESEARCHER, AND MASTER ARCH-AEOLOGICAL NIT-PICKER!

HOW MANY TIMES MUST I *TELL* YOU, MR. McDUCK, THAT JUNIOR WOODCHUCK GUIDEBOOKS ARE *NOT FOR SALE!* THEY ARE FOR USE BY *MEMBERS ONLY!*

SO I'LL JOIN!

AS A *SENIOR* WOODCHUCK? NO, YOU MUST *FIRST* BE A *JUNIOR* WOODCHUCK, AND I SUSPECT YOU SURPASSED THE *AGE LIMITATION* AROUND THE TURN OF THE CENTURY!

>SNORT!<

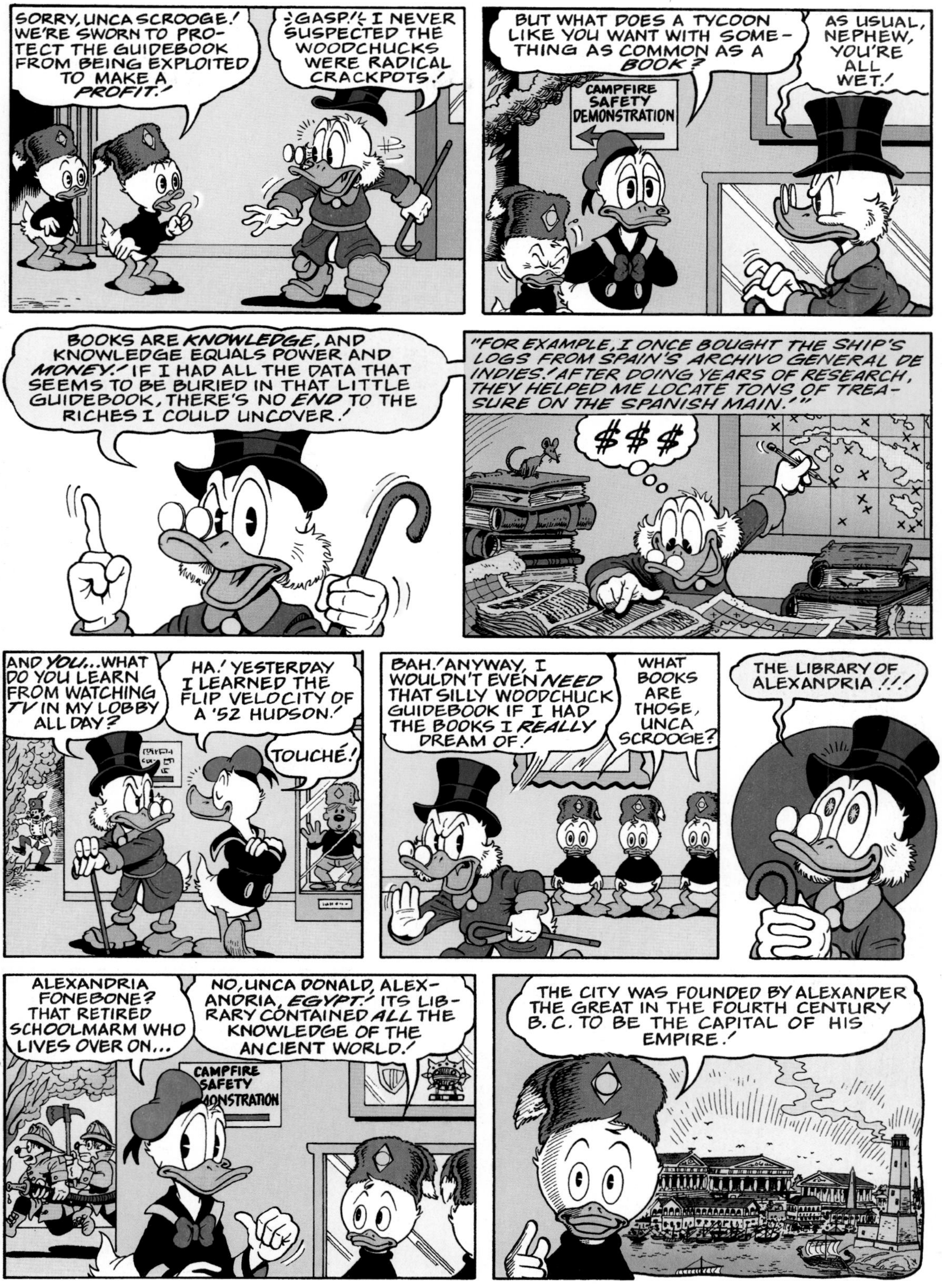
SORRY, UNCA SCROOGE! WE'RE SWORN TO PROTECT THE GUIDEBOOK FROM BEING EXPLOITED TO MAKE A PROFIT!
GASP! I NEVER SUSPECTED THE WOODCHUCKS WERE RADICAL CRACKPOTS!
BUT WHAT DOES A TYCOON LIKE YOU WANT WITH SOMETHING AS COMMON AS A BOOK?
AS USUAL, NEPHEW, YOU'RE ALL WET!
CAMPFIRE SAFETY DEMONSTRATION
BOOKS ARE KNOWLEDGE, AND KNOWLEDGE EQUALS POWER AND MONEY! IF I HAD ALL THE DATA THAT SEEMS TO BE BURIED IN THAT LITTLE GUIDEBOOK, THERE'S NO END TO THE RICHES I COULD UNCOVER!
"FOR EXAMPLE, I ONCE BOUGHT THE SHIP'S LOGS FROM SPAIN'S ARCHIVO GENERAL DE INDIES! AFTER DOING YEARS OF RESEARCH, THEY HELPED ME LOCATE TONS OF TREASURE ON THE SPANISH MAIN!"
$$$
AND YOU... WHAT DO YOU LEARN FROM WATCHING TV IN MY LOBBY ALL DAY?
HA! YESTERDAY I LEARNED THE FLIP VELOCITY OF A '52 HUDSON!
TOUCHÉ!
BAH! ANYWAY, I WOULDN'T EVEN NEED THAT SILLY WOODCHUCK GUIDEBOOK IF I HAD THE BOOKS I REALLY DREAM OF!
WHAT BOOKS ARE THOSE, UNCA SCROOGE?
THE LIBRARY OF ALEXANDRIA!!!
ALEXANDRIA FONEBONE? THAT RETIRED SCHOOLMARM WHO LIVES OVER ON...
NO, UNCA DONALD, ALEXANDRIA, EGYPT! ITS LIBRARY CONTAINED ALL THE KNOWLEDGE OF THE ANCIENT WORLD!
CAMPFIRE SAFETY DEMONSTRATION
THE CITY WAS FOUNDED BY ALEXANDER THE GREAT IN THE FOURTH CENTURY B.C. TO BE THE CAPITAL OF HIS EMPIRE!

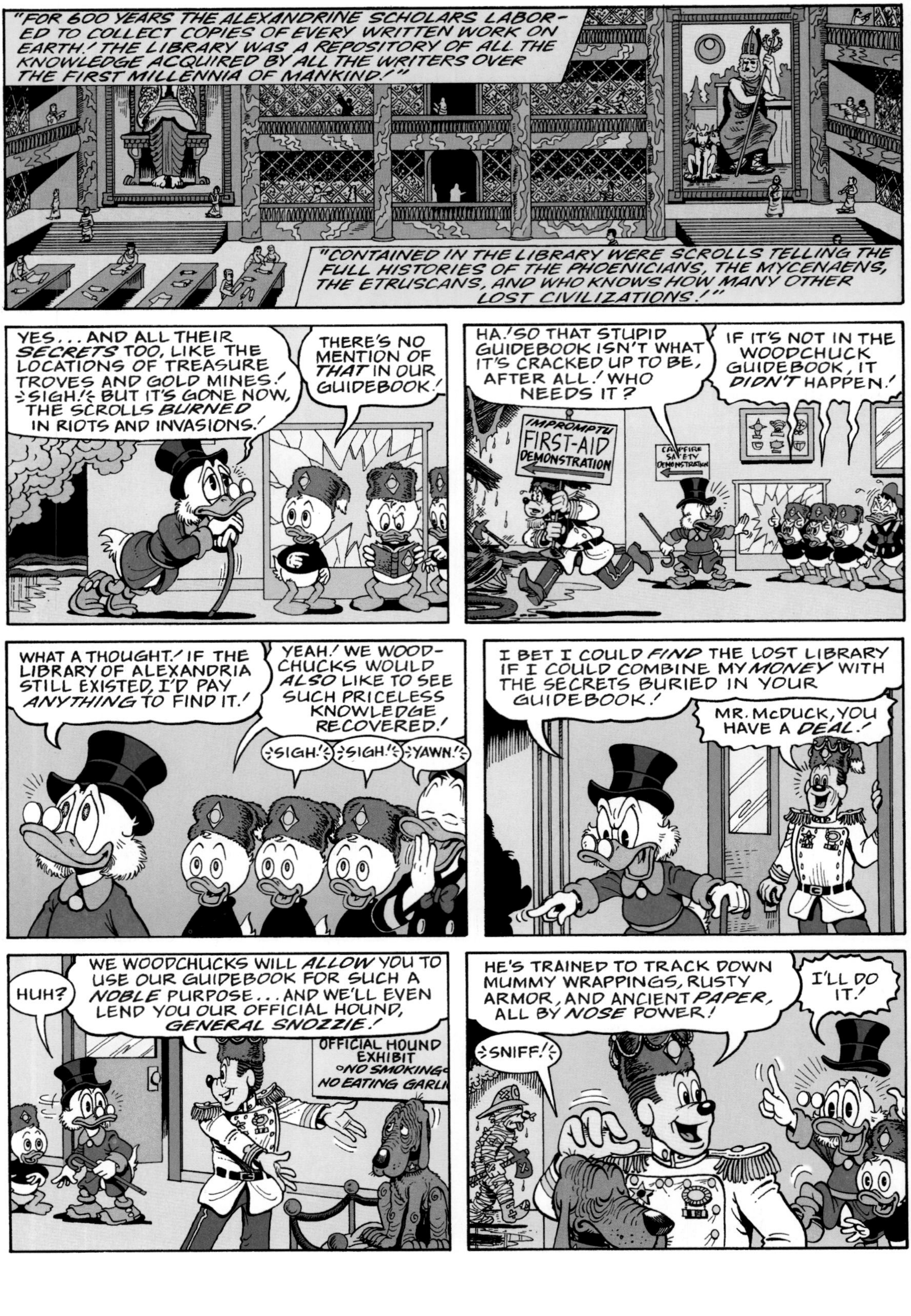
"FOR 600 YEARS THE ALEXANDRINE SCHOLARS LABORED TO COLLECT COPIES OF EVERY WRITTEN WORK ON EARTH! THE LIBRARY WAS A REPOSITORY OF ALL THE KNOWLEDGE ACQUIRED BY ALL THE WRITERS OVER THE FIRST MILLENNIA OF MANKIND!"
"CONTAINED IN THE LIBRARY WERE SCROLLS TELLING THE FULL HISTORIES OF THE PHOENICIANS, THE MYCENAENS, THE ETRUSCANS, AND WHO KNOWS HOW MANY OTHER LOST CIVILIZATIONS!"
YES... AND ALL THEIR SECRETS TOO, LIKE THE LOCATIONS OF TREASURE TROVES AND GOLD MINES! SIGH! BUT IT'S GONE NOW, THE SCROLLS BURNED IN RIOTS AND INVASIONS!
THERE'S NO MENTION OF THAT IN OUR GUIDEBOOK!
HA! SO THAT STUPID GUIDEBOOK ISN'T WHAT IT'S CRACKED UP TO BE, AFTER ALL! WHO NEEDS IT?
IF IT'S NOT IN THE WOODCHUCK GUIDEBOOK, IT DIDN'T HAPPEN!
IMPROMPTU FIRST-AID DEMONSTRATION
CAMPFIRE SAFETY DEMONSTRATION
WHAT A THOUGHT! IF THE LIBRARY OF ALEXANDRIA STILL EXISTED, I'D PAY ANYTHING TO FIND IT!
YEAH! WE WOODCHUCKS WOULD ALSO LIKE TO SEE SUCH PRICELESS KNOWLEDGE RECOVERED!
SIGH!
SIGH!
YAWN!
I BET I COULD FIND THE LOST LIBRARY IF I COULD COMBINE MY MONEY WITH THE SECRETS BURIED IN YOUR GUIDEBOOK!
MR. McDUCK, YOU HAVE A DEAL!
HUH?
WE WOODCHUCKS WILL ALLOW YOU TO USE OUR GUIDEBOOK FOR SUCH A NOBLE PURPOSE... AND WE'LL EVEN LEND YOU OUR OFFICIAL HOUND, GENERAL SNOZZIE!
OFFICIAL HOUND EXHIBIT
NO SMOKING
NO EATING GARLI
HE'S TRAINED TO TRACK DOWN MUMMY WRAPPINGS, RUSTY ARMOR, AND ANCIENT PAPER, ALL BY NOSE POWER!
SNIFF!
I'LL DO IT!

35674044017266

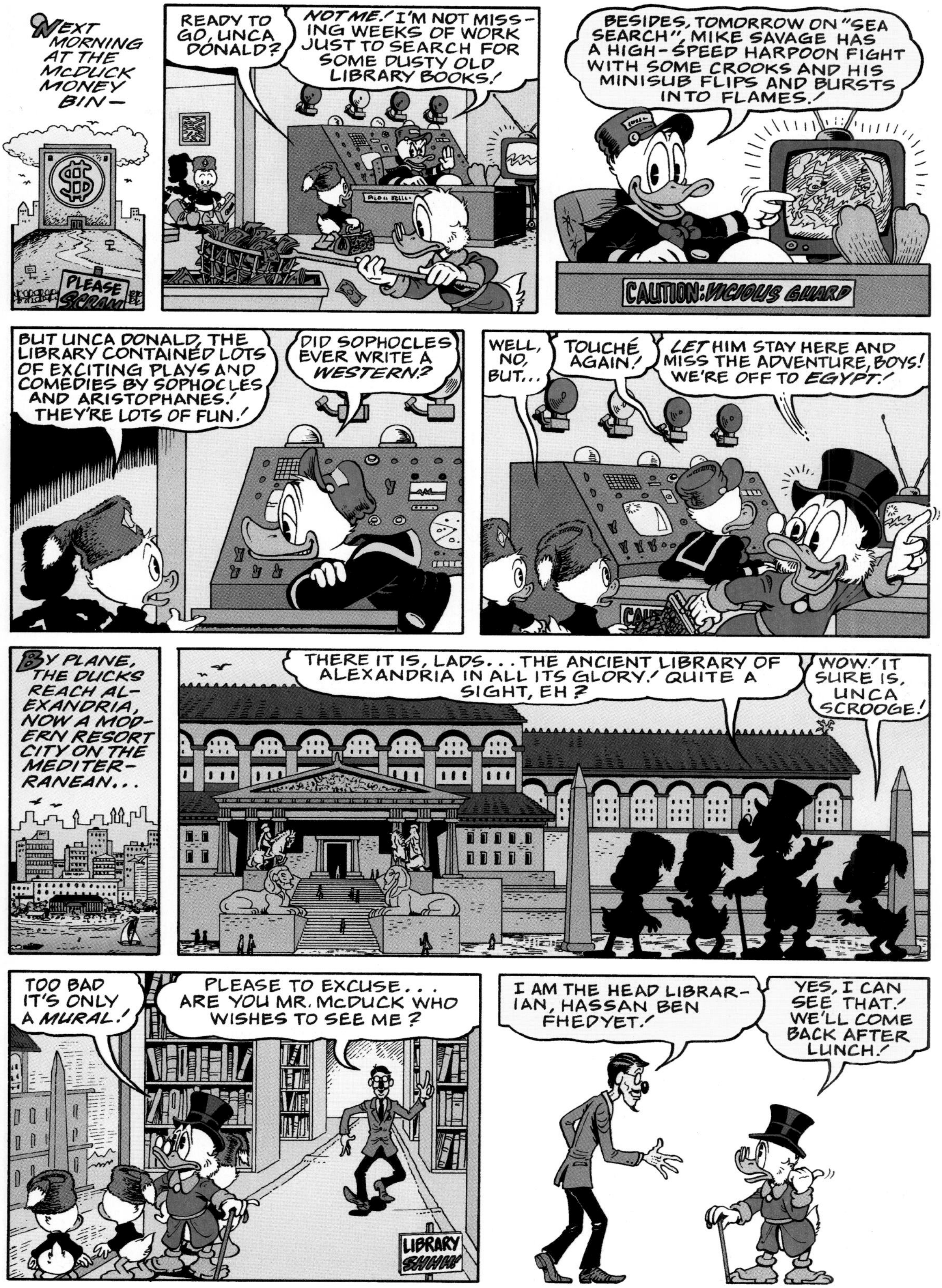

NEXT MORNING AT THE McDUCK MONEY BIN—
PLEASE SCRAM
READY TO GO, UNCA DONALD?
NOT ME! I'M NOT MISSING WEEKS OF WORK JUST TO SEARCH FOR SOME DUSTY OLD LIBRARY BOOKS!
BESIDES, TOMORROW ON "SEA SEARCH", MIKE SAVAGE HAS A HIGH-SPEED HARPOON FIGHT WITH SOME CROOKS AND HIS MINISUB FLIPS AND BURSTS INTO FLAMES!
CAUTION: VICIOUS GUARD
BUT UNCA DONALD, THE LIBRARY CONTAINED LOTS OF EXCITING PLAYS AND COMEDIES BY SOPHOCLES AND ARISTOPHANES! THEY'RE LOTS OF FUN!
DID SOPHOCLES EVER WRITE A WESTERN?
WELL, NO, BUT...
TOUCHÉ AGAIN!
LET HIM STAY HERE AND MISS THE ADVENTURE, BOYS! WE'RE OFF TO EGYPT!
BY PLANE, THE DUCKS REACH ALEXANDRIA, NOW A MODERN RESORT CITY ON THE MEDITERRANEAN...
THERE IT IS, LADS... THE ANCIENT LIBRARY OF ALEXANDRIA IN ALL ITS GLORY! QUITE A SIGHT, EH?
WOW! IT SURE IS, UNCA SCROOGE!
TOO BAD IT'S ONLY A MURAL!
PLEASE TO EXCUSE... ARE YOU MR. McDUCK WHO WISHES TO SEE ME?
LIBRARY SHHH!
I AM THE HEAD LIBRARIAN, HASSAN BEN FHEDYET!
YES, I CAN SEE THAT! WE'LL COME BACK AFTER LUNCH!

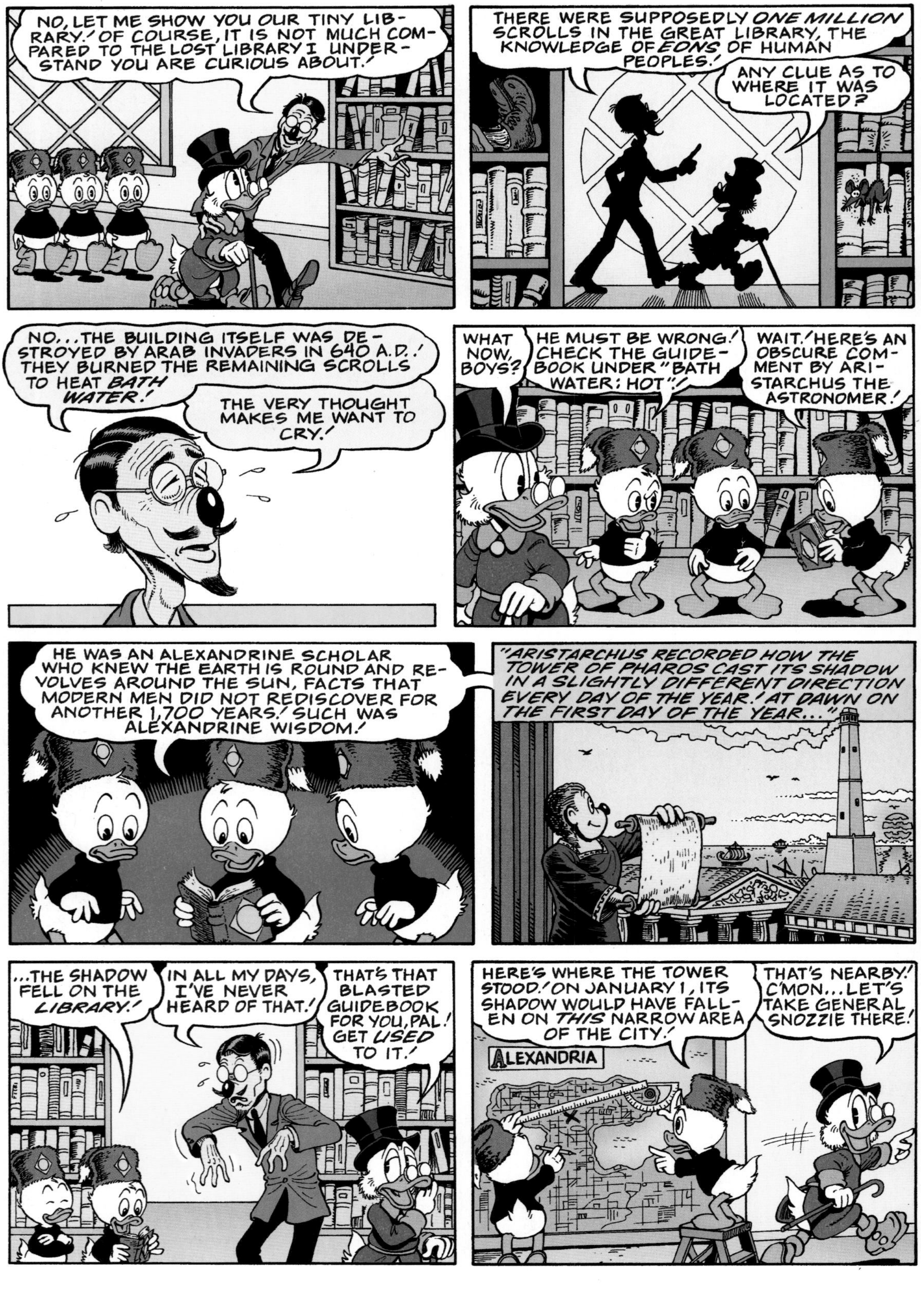
NO, LET ME SHOW YOU OUR TINY LIBRARY! OF COURSE, IT IS NOT MUCH COMPARED TO THE LOST LIBRARY I UNDERSTAND YOU ARE CURIOUS ABOUT!
THERE WERE SUPPOSEDLY *ONE MILLION* SCROLLS IN THE GREAT LIBRARY, THE KNOWLEDGE OF *EONS* OF HUMAN PEOPLES!
ANY CLUE AS TO WHERE IT WAS LOCATED?
NO...THE BUILDING ITSELF WAS DESTROYED BY ARAB INVADERS IN 640 A.D.! THEY BURNED THE REMAINING SCROLLS TO HEAT *BATH WATER!*
THE VERY THOUGHT MAKES ME WANT TO CRY!
WHAT NOW, BOYS?
HE MUST BE WRONG! CHECK THE GUIDEBOOK UNDER "BATH WATER: HOT"!
WAIT! HERE'S AN OBSCURE COMMENT BY ARISTARCHUS THE ASTRONOMER!
HE WAS AN ALEXANDRINE SCHOLAR WHO KNEW THE EARTH IS ROUND AND REVOLVES AROUND THE SUN, FACTS THAT MODERN MEN DID NOT REDISCOVER FOR ANOTHER 1,700 YEARS! SUCH WAS ALEXANDRINE WISDOM!
"ARISTARCHUS RECORDED HOW THE TOWER OF PHAROS CAST ITS SHADOW IN A SLIGHTLY DIFFERENT DIRECTION EVERY DAY OF THE YEAR! AT DAWN ON THE FIRST DAY OF THE YEAR..."
...THE SHADOW FELL ON THE *LIBRARY!*
IN ALL MY DAYS, I'VE NEVER HEARD OF THAT!
THAT'S THAT BLASTED GUIDEBOOK FOR YOU, PAL! GET *USED* TO IT!
HERE'S WHERE THE TOWER STOOD! ON JANUARY 1, ITS SHADOW WOULD HAVE FALLEN ON *THIS* NARROW AREA OF THE CITY!
ALEXANDRIA
THAT'S NEARBY! C'MON...LET'S TAKE GENERAL SNOZZIE THERE!

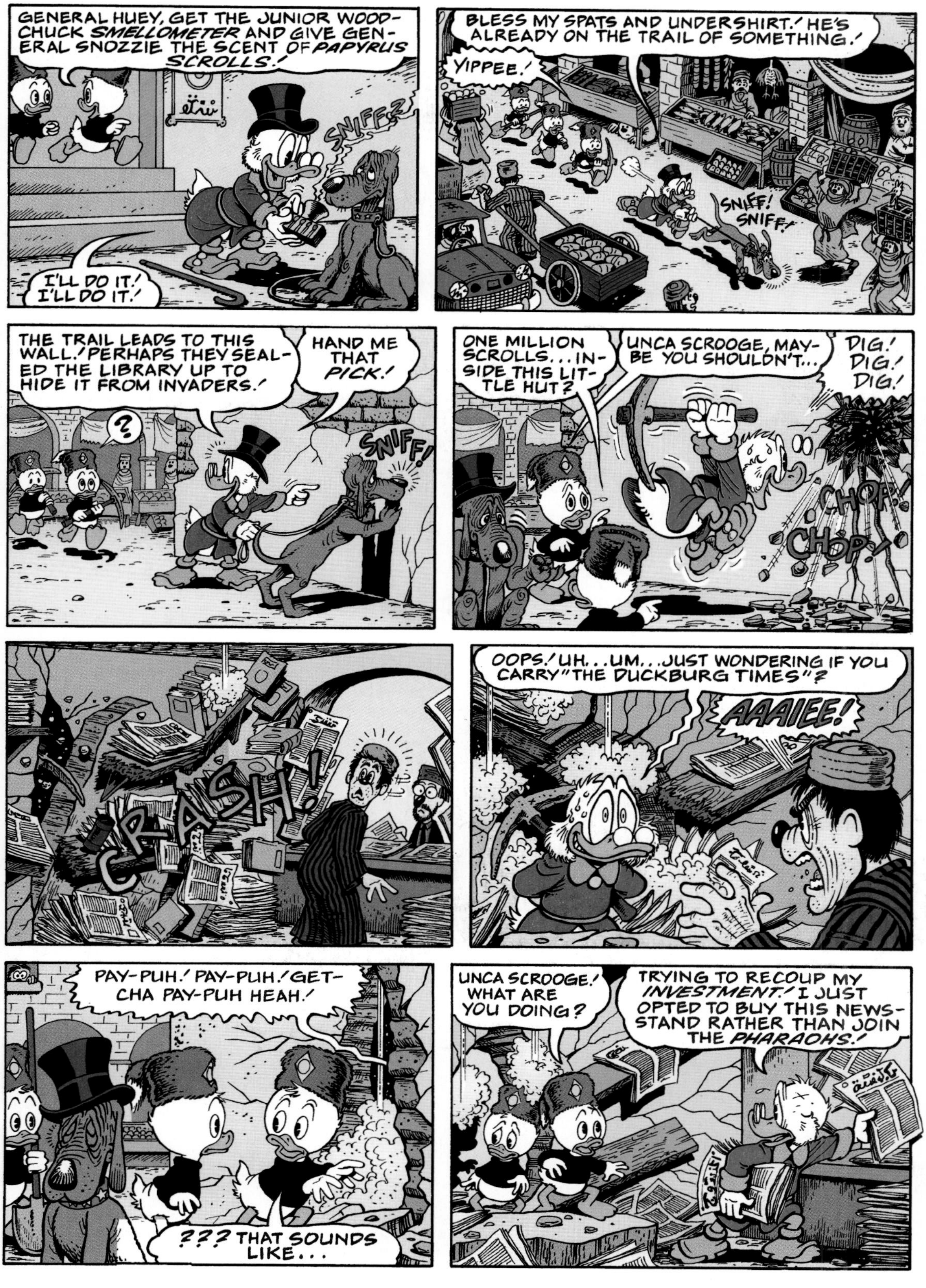
GENERAL HUEY, GET THE JUNIOR WOODCHUCK SMELLOMETER AND GIVE GENERAL SNOZZIE THE SCENT OF PAPYRUS SCROLLS!
SNIFF?
I'LL DO IT! I'LL DO IT!
BLESS MY SPATS AND UNDERSHIRT! HE'S ALREADY ON THE TRAIL OF SOMETHING!
YIPPEE!
SNIFF! SNIFF!
THE TRAIL LEADS TO THIS WALL! PERHAPS THEY SEALED THE LIBRARY UP TO HIDE IT FROM INVADERS!
HAND ME THAT PICK!
?
SNIFF!
ONE MILLION SCROLLS... INSIDE THIS LITTLE HUT?
UNCA SCROOGE, MAYBE YOU SHOULDN'T...
DIG! DIG! DIG!
CHOP! CHOP!
CRASH!
OOPS! UH...UM...JUST WONDERING IF YOU CARRY "THE DUCKBURG TIMES"?
AAAIEE!
PAY-PUH! PAY-PUH! GET-CHA PAY-PUH HEAH!
??? THAT SOUNDS LIKE...
UNCA SCROOGE! WHAT ARE YOU DOING?
TRYING TO RECOUP MY INVESTMENT! I JUST OPTED TO BUY THIS NEWSSTAND RATHER THAN JOIN THE PHARAOHS!

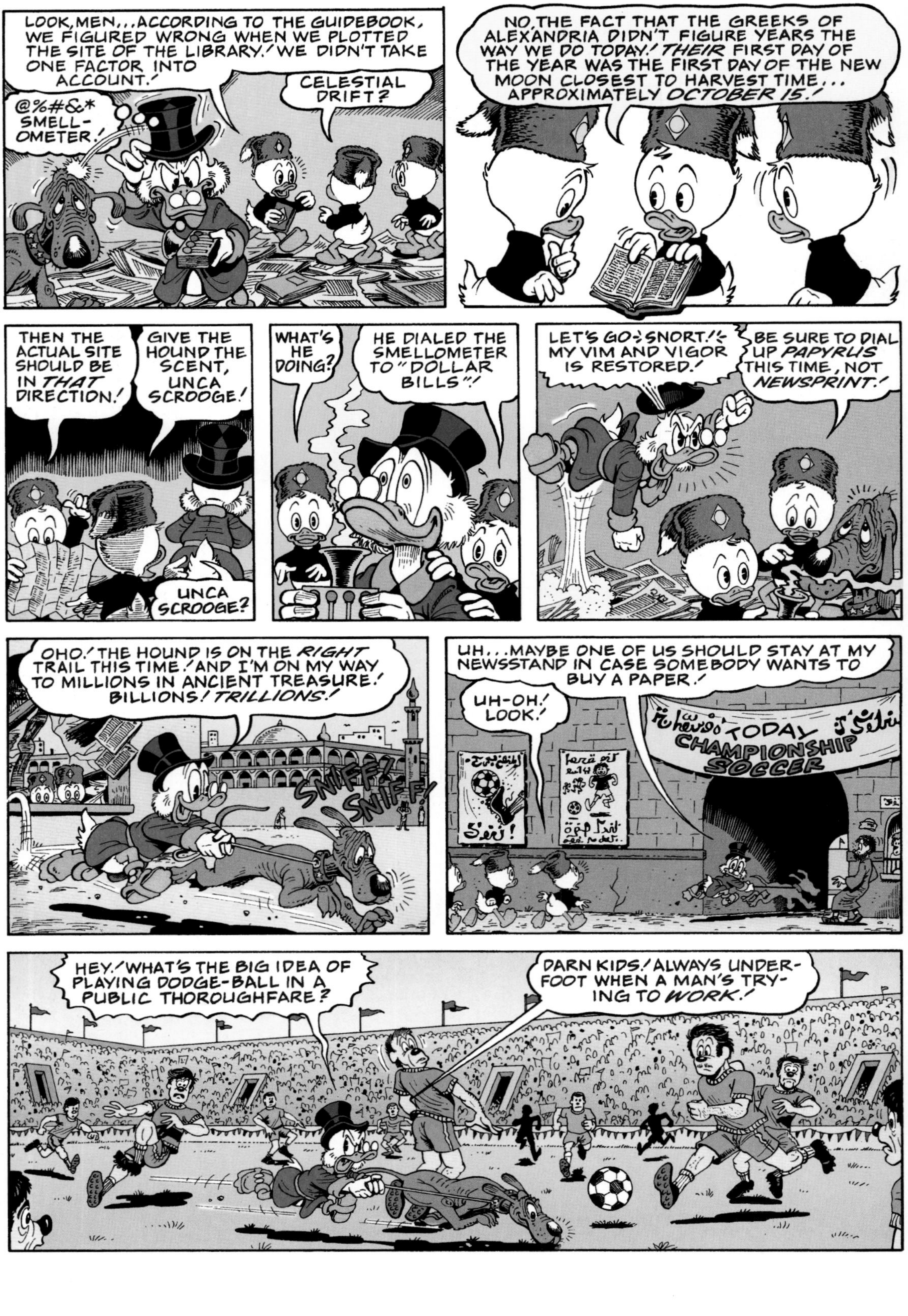
LOOK, MEN,.. ACCORDING TO THE GUIDEBOOK, WE FIGURED WRONG WHEN WE PLOTTED THE SITE OF THE LIBRARY! WE DIDN'T TAKE ONE FACTOR INTO ACCOUNT!
@%#&* SMELL-OMETER!
CELESTIAL DRIFT?
NO, THE FACT THAT THE GREEKS OF ALEXANDRIA DIDN'T FIGURE YEARS THE WAY WE DO TODAY! THEIR FIRST DAY OF THE YEAR WAS THE FIRST DAY OF THE NEW MOON CLOSEST TO HARVEST TIME... APPROXIMATELY OCTOBER 15!
THEN THE ACTUAL SITE SHOULD BE IN THAT DIRECTION!
GIVE THE HOUND THE SCENT, UNCA SCROOGE!
UNCA SCROOGE?
WHAT'S HE DOING?
HE DIALED THE SMELLOMETER TO "DOLLAR BILLS"!
LET'S GO! SNORT! MY VIM AND VIGOR IS RESTORED!
BE SURE TO DIAL UP PAPYRUS THIS TIME, NOT NEWSPRINT!
OHO! THE HOUND IS ON THE RIGHT TRAIL THIS TIME! AND I'M ON MY WAY TO MILLIONS IN ANCIENT TREASURE! BILLIONS! TRILLIONS!
SNIFF! SNIFF!
UH... MAYBE ONE OF US SHOULD STAY AT MY NEWSSTAND IN CASE SOMEBODY WANTS TO BUY A PAPER!
UH-OH! LOOK!
TODAY CHAMPIONSHIP SOCCER
HEY! WHAT'S THE BIG IDEA OF PLAYING DODGE-BALL IN A PUBLIC THOROUGHFARE?
DARN KIDS! ALWAYS UNDER-FOOT WHEN A MAN'S TRY-ING TO WORK!

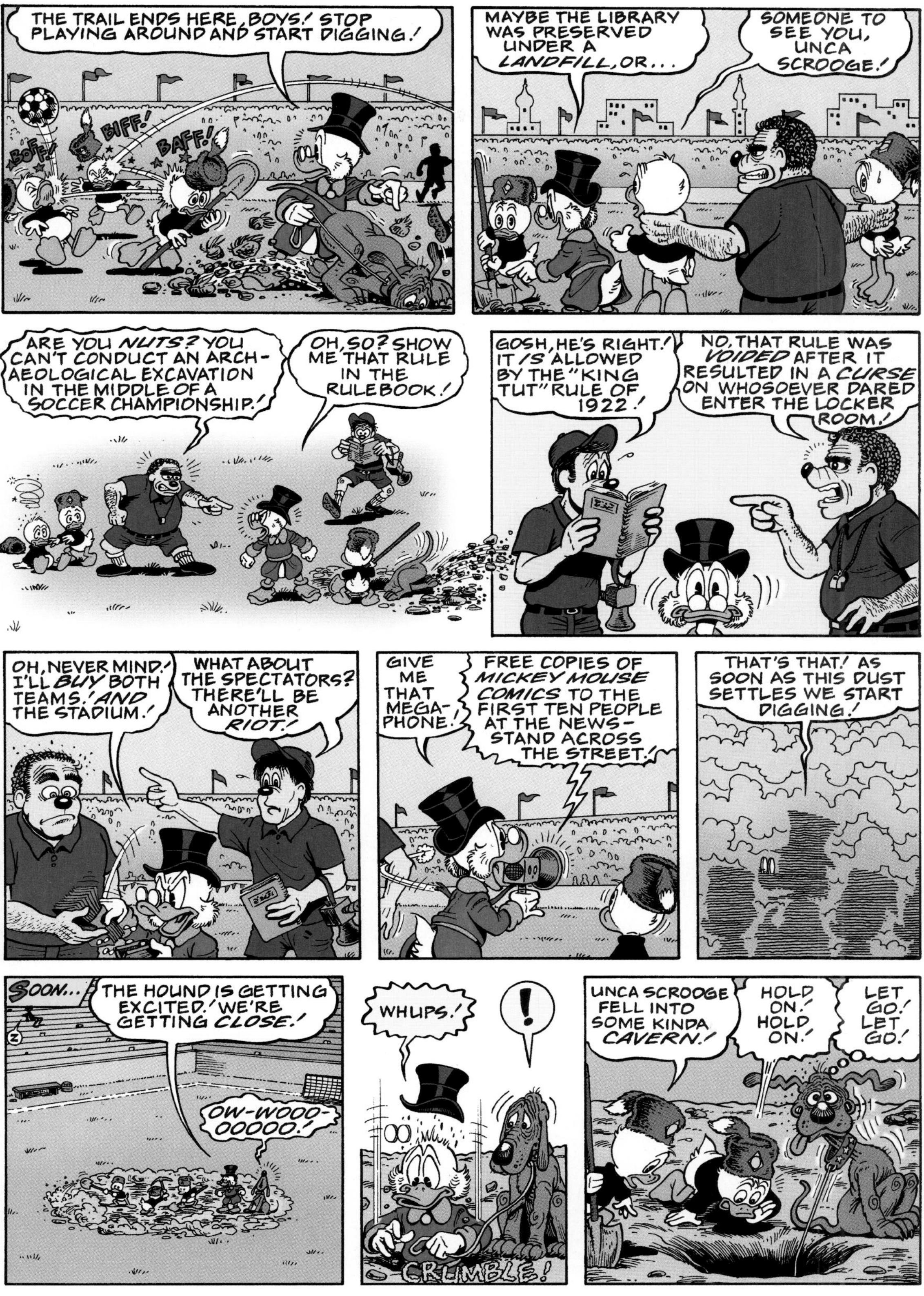
THE TRAIL ENDS HERE, BOYS! STOP PLAYING AROUND AND START DIGGING!
BOFF!
BIFF!
BAFF!
MAYBE THE LIBRARY WAS PRESERVED UNDER A LANDFILL, OR...
SOMEONE TO SEE YOU, UNCA SCROOGE!
ARE YOU NUTS? YOU CAN'T CONDUCT AN ARCHAEOLOGICAL EXCAVATION IN THE MIDDLE OF A SOCCER CHAMPIONSHIP!
OH, SO? SHOW ME THAT RULE IN THE RULEBOOK!
GOSH, HE'S RIGHT! IT IS ALLOWED BY THE "KING TUT" RULE OF 1922!
NO, THAT RULE WAS VOIDED AFTER IT RESULTED IN A CURSE ON WHOSOEVER DARED ENTER THE LOCKER ROOM!
OH, NEVER MIND! I'LL BUY BOTH TEAMS! AND THE STADIUM!
WHAT ABOUT THE SPECTATORS? THERE'LL BE ANOTHER RIOT!
GIVE ME THAT MEGAPHONE!
FREE COPIES OF MICKEY MOUSE COMICS TO THE FIRST TEN PEOPLE AT THE NEWSSTAND ACROSS THE STREET!
THAT'S THAT! AS SOON AS THIS DUST SETTLES WE START DIGGING!
SOON...
THE HOUND IS GETTING EXCITED! WE'RE GETTING CLOSE!
OW-WOOO-OOOOO!
WHUPS!
!
CRUMBLE!
UNCA SCROOGE FELL INTO SOME KINDA CAVERN!
HOLD ON! HOLD ON!
LET GO! LET GO!

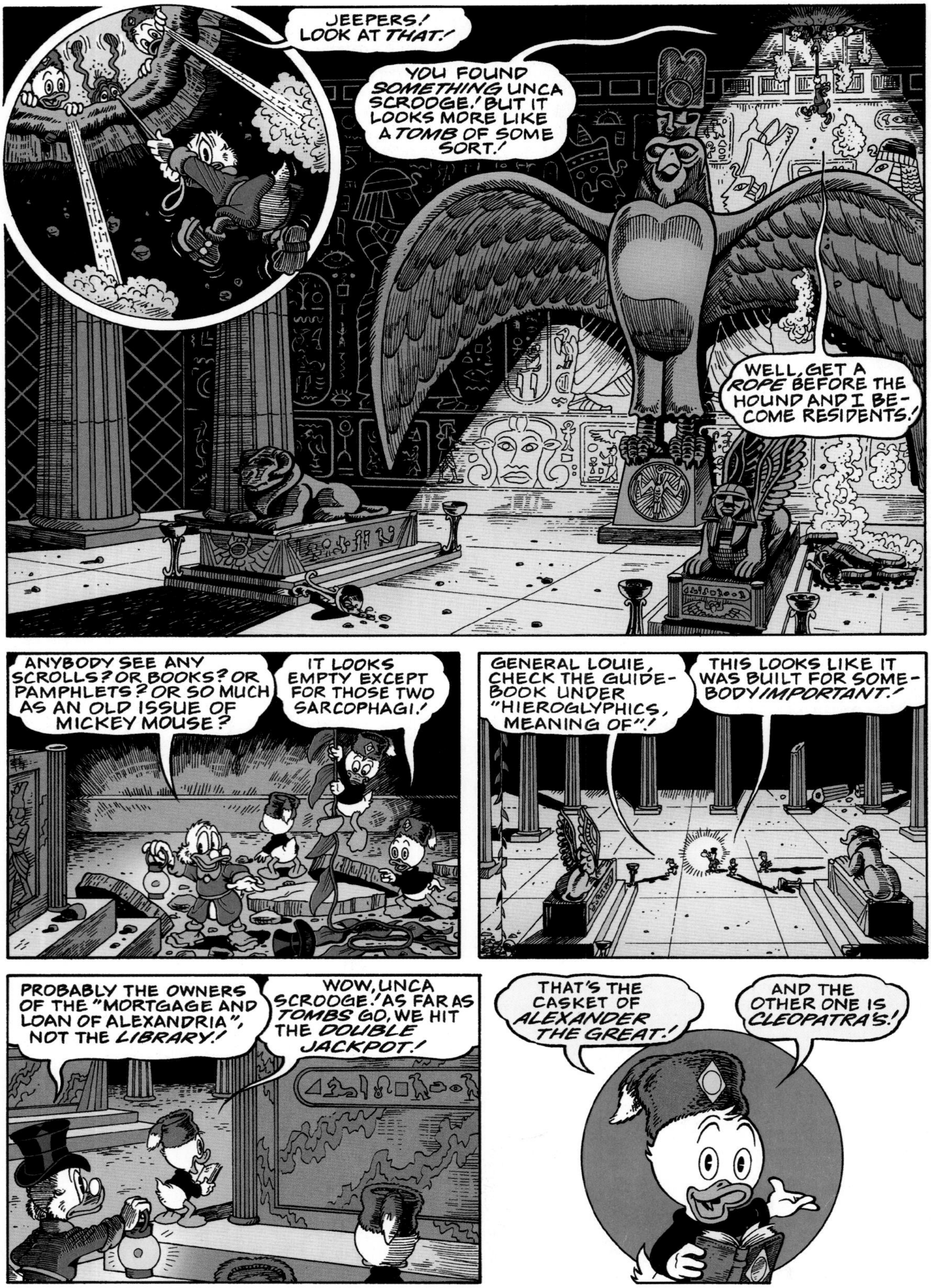
JEEPERS! LOOK AT *THAT!*
YOU FOUND *SOMETHING* UNCA SCROOGE! BUT IT LOOKS MORE LIKE A *TOMB* OF SOME SORT!
WELL, GET A *ROPE* BEFORE THE HOUND AND I BE-COME RESIDENTS!
ANYBODY SEE ANY SCROLLS? OR BOOKS? OR PAMPHLETS? OR SO MUCH AS AN OLD ISSUE OF MICKEY MOUSE?
IT LOOKS EMPTY EXCEPT FOR THOSE TWO SARCOPHAGI!
GENERAL LOUIE, CHECK THE GUIDE-BOOK UNDER "HIEROGLYPHICS, MEANING OF"!
THIS LOOKS LIKE IT WAS BUILT FOR SOME-BODY *IMPORTANT!*
PROBABLY THE OWNERS OF THE "MORTGAGE AND LOAN OF ALEXANDRIA", NOT THE *LIBRARY!*
WOW, UNCA SCROOGE! AS FAR AS *TOMBS* GO, WE HIT THE *DOUBLE JACKPOT!*
THAT'S THE CASKET OF *ALEXANDER THE GREAT!*
AND THE OTHER ONE IS *CLEOPATRA'S!*

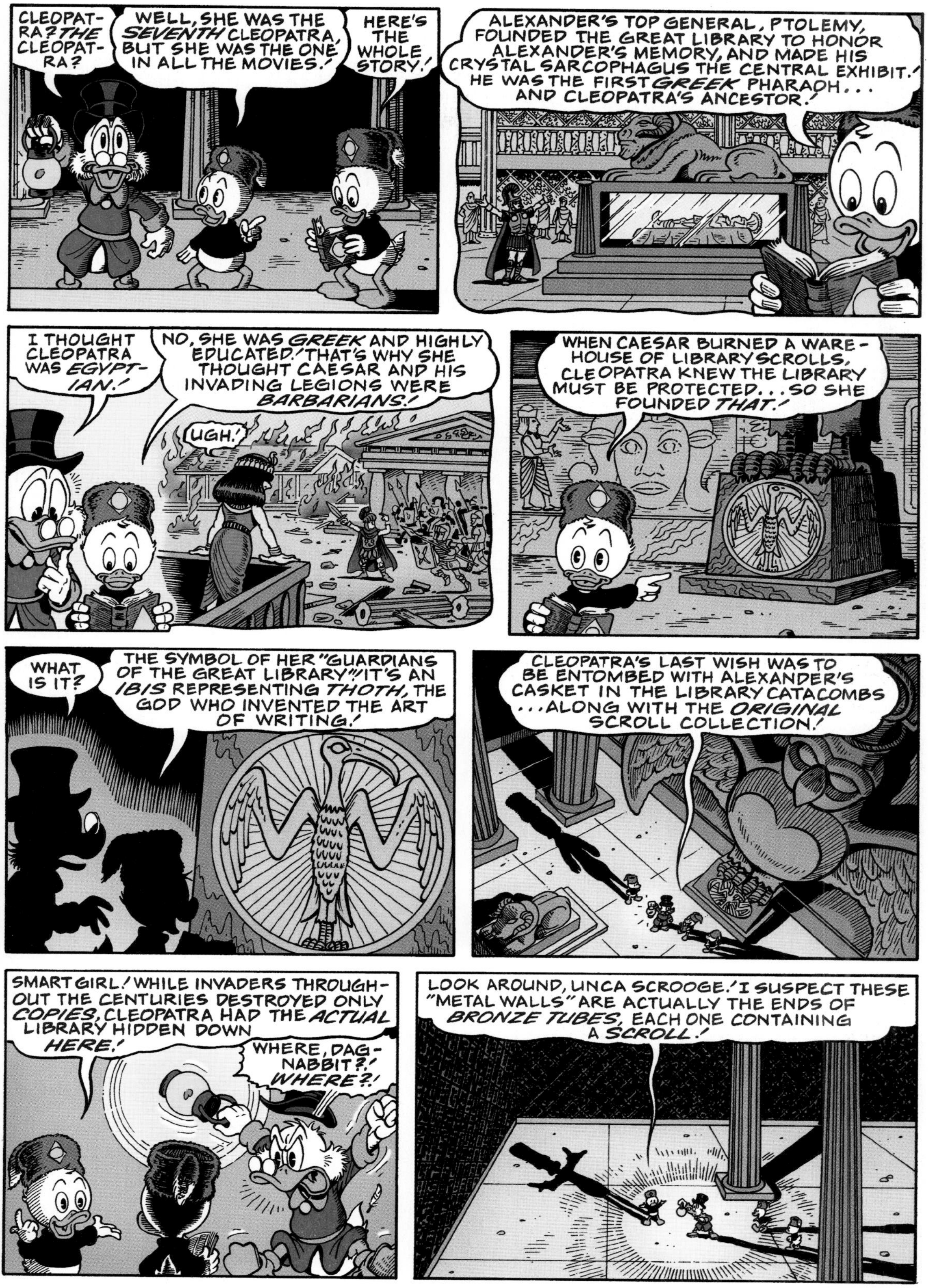
CLEOPATRA? THE CLEOPATRA?
WELL, SHE WAS THE SEVENTH CLEOPATRA, BUT SHE WAS THE ONE IN ALL THE MOVIES!
HERE'S THE WHOLE STORY!
ALEXANDER'S TOP GENERAL, PTOLEMY, FOUNDED THE GREAT LIBRARY TO HONOR ALEXANDER'S MEMORY, AND MADE HIS CRYSTAL SARCOPHAGUS THE CENTRAL EXHIBIT! HE WAS THE FIRST GREEK PHARAOH... AND CLEOPATRA'S ANCESTOR!
I THOUGHT CLEOPATRA WAS EGYPTIAN!
NO, SHE WAS GREEK AND HIGHLY EDUCATED! THAT'S WHY SHE THOUGHT CAESAR AND HIS INVADING LEGIONS WERE BARBARIANS!
UGH!
WHEN CAESAR BURNED A WAREHOUSE OF LIBRARY SCROLLS, CLEOPATRA KNEW THE LIBRARY MUST BE PROTECTED... SO SHE FOUNDED THAT!
WHAT IS IT?
THE SYMBOL OF HER "GUARDIANS OF THE GREAT LIBRARY"! IT'S AN IBIS REPRESENTING THOTH, THE GOD WHO INVENTED THE ART OF WRITING!
CLEOPATRA'S LAST WISH WAS TO BE ENTOMBED WITH ALEXANDER'S CASKET IN THE LIBRARY CATACOMBS ...ALONG WITH THE ORIGINAL SCROLL COLLECTION!
SMART GIRL! WHILE INVADERS THROUGHOUT THE CENTURIES DESTROYED ONLY COPIES, CLEOPATRA HAD THE ACTUAL LIBRARY HIDDEN DOWN HERE!
WHERE, DAGNABBIT?! WHERE?!
LOOK AROUND, UNCA SCROOGE! I SUSPECT THESE "METAL WALLS" ARE ACTUALLY THE ENDS OF BRONZE TUBES, EACH ONE CONTAINING A SCROLL!

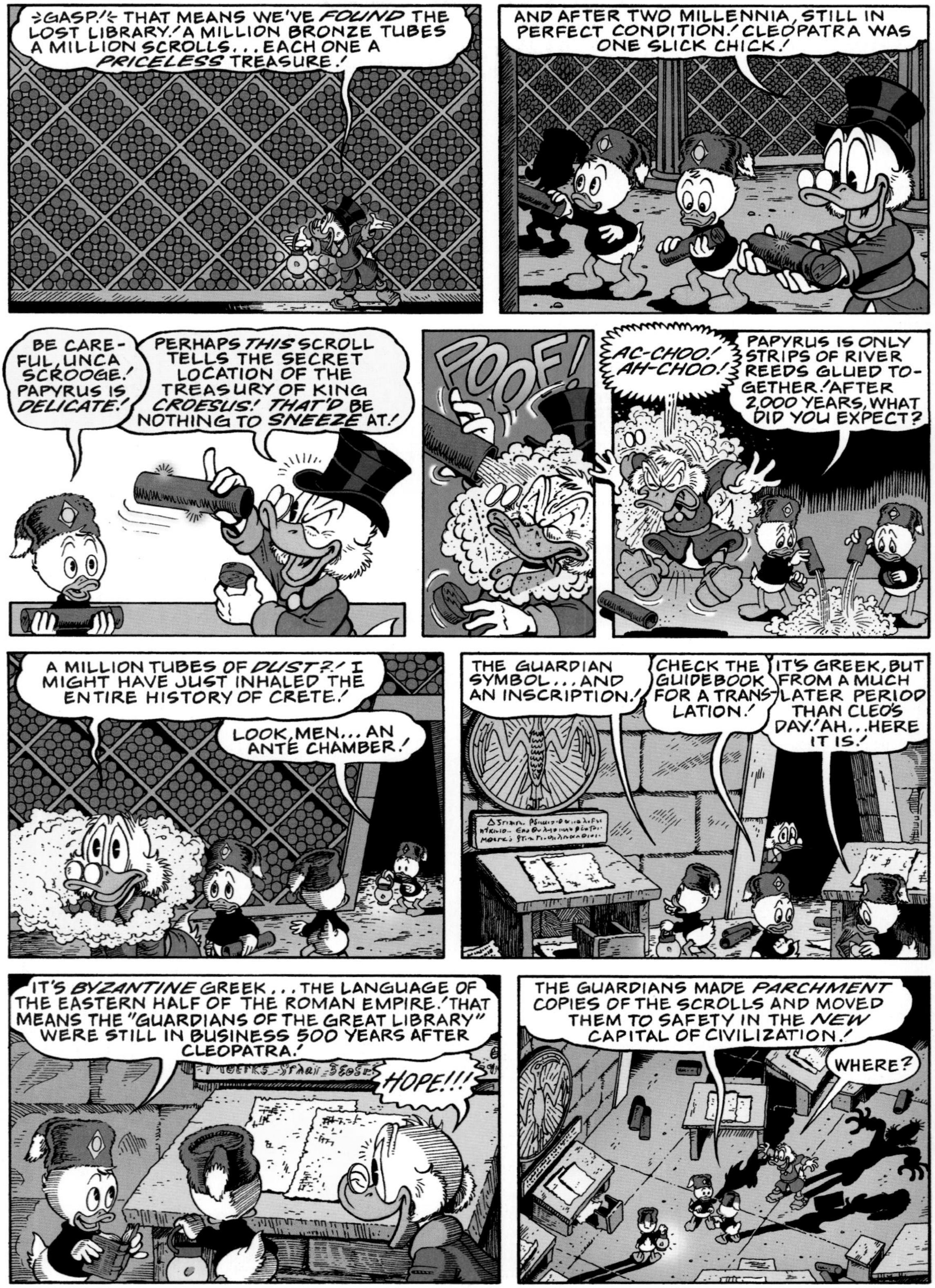

≥GASP!≤ THAT MEANS WE'VE FOUND THE LOST LIBRARY! A MILLION BRONZE TUBES A MILLION SCROLLS. . . EACH ONE A PRICELESS TREASURE!
AND AFTER TWO MILLENNIA, STILL IN PERFECT CONDITION! CLEOPATRA WAS ONE SLICK CHICK!
BE CARE-FUL, UNCA SCROOGE! PAPYRUS IS DELICATE!
PERHAPS THIS SCROLL TELLS THE SECRET LOCATION OF THE TREASURY OF KING CROESUS! THAT'D BE NOTHING TO SNEEZE AT!
POOF!
AC-CHOO! AH-CHOO!
PAPYRUS IS ONLY STRIPS OF RIVER REEDS GLUED TO-GETHER! AFTER 2,000 YEARS, WHAT DID YOU EXPECT?
A MILLION TUBES OF DUST?! I MIGHT HAVE JUST INHALED THE ENTIRE HISTORY OF CRETE!
LOOK, MEN... AN ANTE CHAMBER!
THE GUARDIAN SYMBOL... AND AN INSCRIPTION!
CHECK THE GUIDEBOOK FOR A TRANS-LATION!
IT'S GREEK, BUT FROM A MUCH LATER PERIOD THAN CLEO'S DAY! AH... HERE IT IS!
IT'S BYZANTINE GREEK... THE LANGUAGE OF THE EASTERN HALF OF THE ROMAN EMPIRE! THAT MEANS THE "GUARDIANS OF THE GREAT LIBRARY" WERE STILL IN BUSINESS 500 YEARS AFTER CLEOPATRA!
HOPE!!!
THE GUARDIANS MADE PARCHMENT COPIES OF THE SCROLLS AND MOVED THEM TO SAFETY IN THE NEW CAPITAL OF CIVILIZATION!
WHERE?

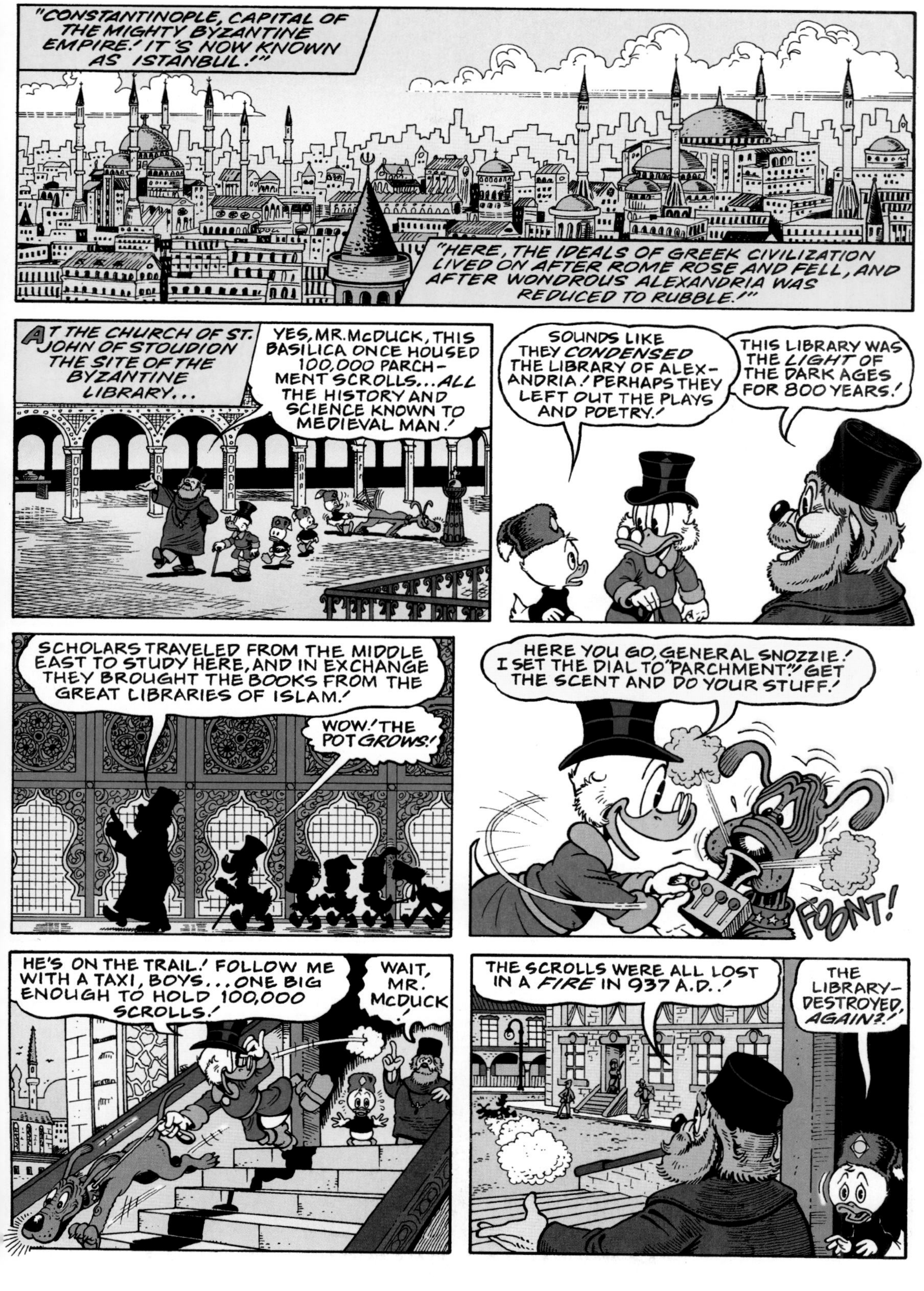
"CONSTANTINOPLE, CAPITAL OF THE MIGHTY BYZANTINE EMPIRE! IT'S NOW KNOWN AS ISTANBUL!"
"HERE, THE IDEALS OF GREEK CIVILIZATION LIVED ON AFTER ROME ROSE AND FELL, AND AFTER WONDROUS ALEXANDRIA WAS REDUCED TO RUBBLE!"
AT THE CHURCH OF ST. JOHN OF STOUDION THE SITE OF THE BYZANTINE LIBRARY...
YES, MR. McDUCK, THIS BASILICA ONCE HOUSED 100,000 PARCHMENT SCROLLS... ALL THE HISTORY AND SCIENCE KNOWN TO MEDIEVAL MAN!
SOUNDS LIKE THEY CONDENSED THE LIBRARY OF ALEXANDRIA! PERHAPS THEY LEFT OUT THE PLAYS AND POETRY!
THIS LIBRARY WAS THE LIGHT OF THE DARK AGES FOR 800 YEARS!
SCHOLARS TRAVELED FROM THE MIDDLE EAST TO STUDY HERE, AND IN EXCHANGE THEY BROUGHT THE BOOKS FROM THE GREAT LIBRARIES OF ISLAM!
WOW! THE POT GROWS!
HERE YOU GO, GENERAL SNOZZIE! I SET THE DIAL TO "PARCHMENT!" GET THE SCENT AND DO YOUR STUFF!
FOONT!
HE'S ON THE TRAIL! FOLLOW ME WITH A TAXI, BOYS... ONE BIG ENOUGH TO HOLD 100,000 SCROLLS!
WAIT, MR. McDUCK!
THE SCROLLS WERE ALL LOST IN A FIRE IN 937 A.D.!
THE LIBRARY-DESTROYED, AGAIN?!

ONLY THE ORIGINALS! THE MONKS IN OUR SCRIPTORIUM HAD SPENT CENTURIES COPYING THE SCROLLS INTO THE LATEST INVENTION...*BOOKS!* TEN SCROLLS FIT IN EACH BOOK!

THOSE 10,000 BOOKS WERE THE PRIDE OF CONSTANTINOPLE ...UNTIL THEY *DISAPPEARED* WHEN THE CITY WAS LOOTED DURING THE 4TH CRUSADE!

YES...HERE IT IS IN THE GUIDE-BOOK!

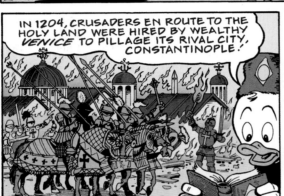

IN 1204, CRUSADERS EN ROUTE TO THE HOLY LAND WERE HIRED BY WEALTHY *VENICE* TO PILLAGE ITS RIVAL CITY, CONSTANTINOPLE!

OUR TRAIL LEADS TO *VENICE!* WHERE'S UNCA SCROOGE?

I CAN'T EVEN SEE HIM! MAYBE WE SHOULD HAVE TOLD HIM THAT PARCHMENT *ISN'T* PAPER...

...IT'S *ANIMAL SKIN!*

@#%@

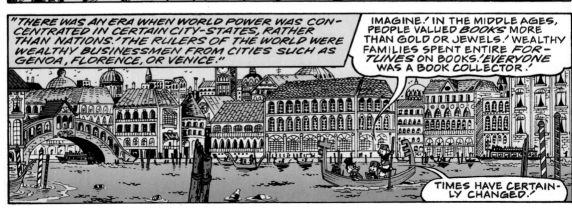

"THERE WAS AN ERA WHEN WORLD POWER WAS CONCENTRATED IN CERTAIN CITY-STATES, RATHER THAN NATIONS! THE RULERS OF THE WORLD WERE WEALTHY *BUSINESSMEN* FROM CITIES SUCH AS GENOA, FLORENCE, OR VENICE."

IMAGINE! IN THE MIDDLE AGES, PEOPLE VALUED *BOOKS* MORE THAN GOLD OR JEWELS! WEALTHY FAMILIES SPENT ENTIRE *FORTUNES* ON BOOKS! *EVERYONE* WAS A BOOK COLLECTOR!

TIMES HAVE CERTAINLY CHANGED!

THE GUIDEBOOK SAYS THAT THE CRUSADERS TOOK THE BYZANTINE LIBRARY TO THE ABBEY OF *SAN SLANTI!*

THAT'S JUST AHEAD! POLE *FASTER!*

HM... THAT MUST BE IT!

THE PLACE IS SINKING INTO THE MUD JUST LIKE ALL OF VENICE HAS BEEN DOING FOR A THOUSAND YEARS!

SHORTLY...

YES, SIGNOR McDUCK, THIS ABBEY ONCE HOUSED A MAGNIFICENT LIBRARY! SOME SAY OUR BOOKS SPARKED THE *RENAISSANCE!*

LEONARDO AND MICHELANGELO GOT THEIR FIRST INSPIRATIONS STUDYING HERE! ANOTHER MAN READ OF THE WONDERS OF THE FAR EAST AND JOURNEYED THERE WITH HIS SON SEEKING RICHES!

AND, ACCORDING TO OUR GUIDEBOOK, THE SON *REPAID* THE LIBRARY BY BRINGING BACK COPIES OF THE GREAT BOOKS OF KUBLAI KHAN'S EMPIRE! HIS NAME WAS *MARCO POLO!*

MARCO POLO ADDED THE LIBRARIES OF ANCIENT *CATHAY* TO THE POT? THIS TREASURE CHEST JUST *TRIPLED* IN VALUE!

BUT WHAT HAPPENED TO ALL THOSE BOOKS?!

COME! I WILL SHOW YOU!

KLONK!

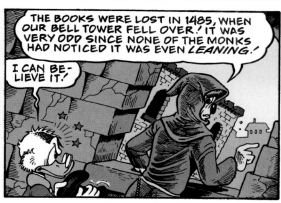

THE BOOKS WERE LOST IN 1485, WHEN OUR BELL TOWER FELL OVER! IT WAS VERY ODD SINCE NONE OF THE MONKS HAD NOTICED IT WAS EVEN *LEANING!*

I CAN BE- LIEVE IT!

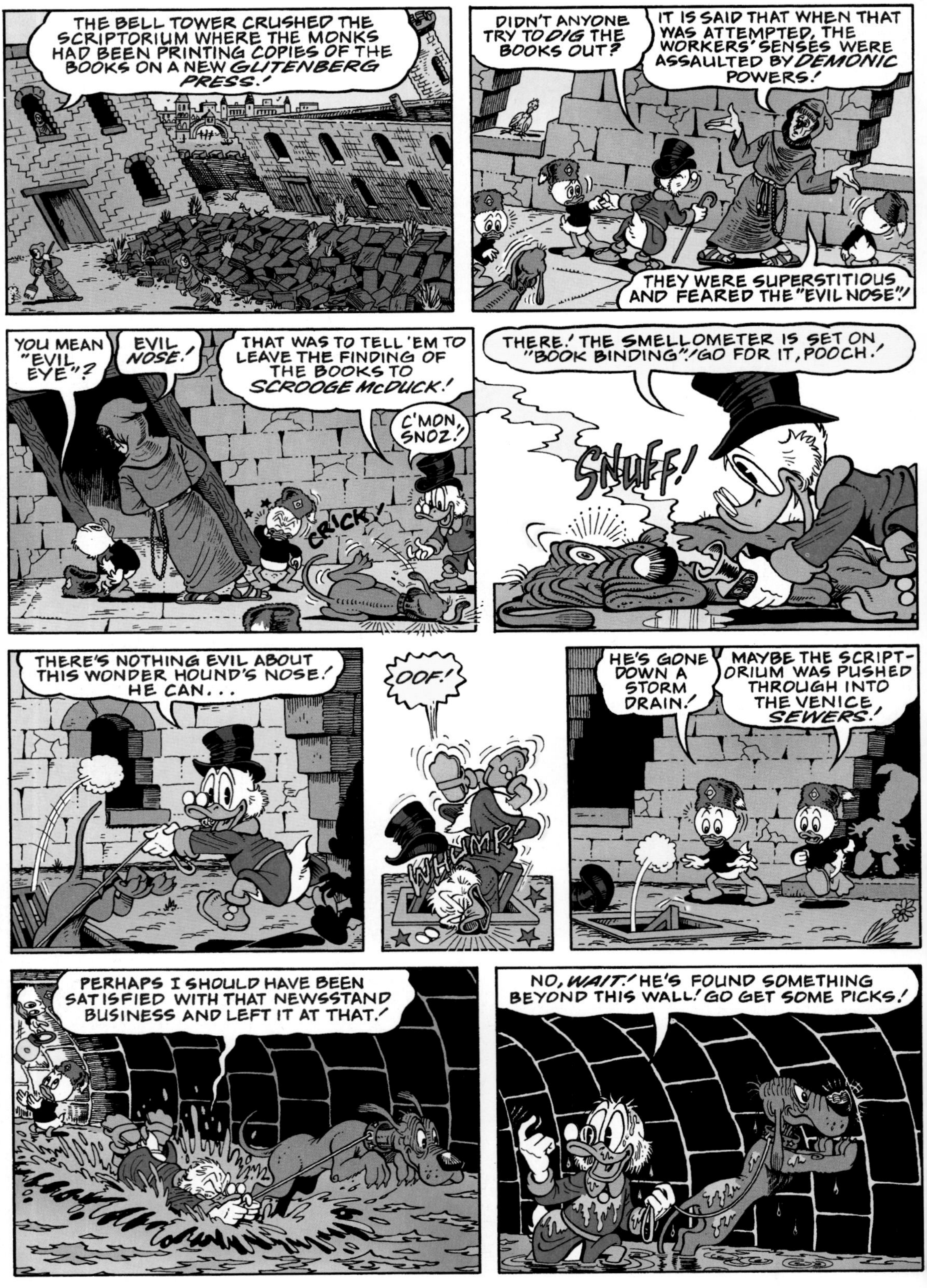
THE BELL TOWER CRUSHED THE SCRIPTORIUM WHERE THE MONKS HAD BEEN PRINTING COPIES OF THE BOOKS ON A NEW GUTENBERG PRESS!
DIDN'T ANYONE TRY TO DIG THE BOOKS OUT?
IT IS SAID THAT WHEN THAT WAS ATTEMPTED, THE WORKERS' SENSES WERE ASSAULTED BY DEMONIC POWERS!
THEY WERE SUPERSTITIOUS AND FEARED THE "EVIL NOSE"!
YOU MEAN "EVIL EYE"?
EVIL NOSE!
THAT WAS TO TELL 'EM TO LEAVE THE FINDING OF THE BOOKS TO SCROOGE McDUCK!
C'MON, SNOZ!
CRICK!
THERE! THE SMELLOMETER IS SET ON "BOOK BINDING"! GO FOR IT, POOCH!
SNUFF!
THERE'S NOTHING EVIL ABOUT THIS WONDER HOUND'S NOSE! HE CAN...
OOF!
WHUMP!
HE'S GONE DOWN A STORM DRAIN!
MAYBE THE SCRIPTORIUM WAS PUSHED THROUGH INTO THE VENICE SEWERS!
PERHAPS I SHOULD HAVE BEEN SATISFIED WITH THAT NEWSSTAND BUSINESS AND LEFT IT AT THAT!
NO, WAIT! HE'S FOUND SOMETHING BEYOND THIS WALL! GO GET SOME PICKS!

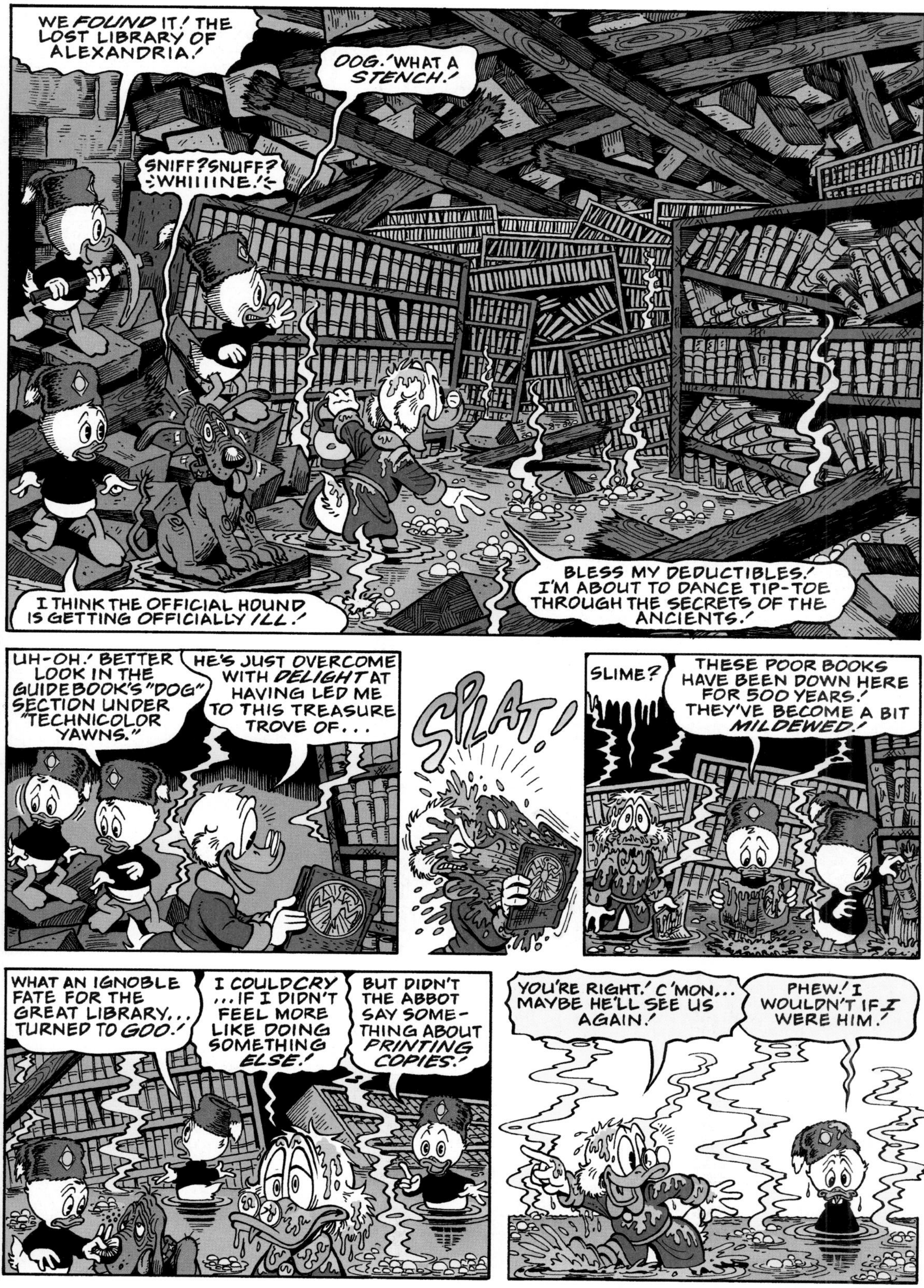
WE FOUND IT! THE LOST LIBRARY OF ALEXANDRIA!
OOG! WHAT A STENCH!
SNIFF? SNUFF? WHIIIINE!
I THINK THE OFFICIAL HOUND IS GETTING OFFICIALLY ILL!
BLESS MY DEDUCTIBLES! I'M ABOUT TO DANCE TIP-TOE THROUGH THE SECRETS OF THE ANCIENTS!
UH-OH! BETTER LOOK IN THE GUIDEBOOK'S "DOG" SECTION UNDER "TECHNICOLOR YAWNS."
HE'S JUST OVERCOME WITH DELIGHT AT HAVING LED ME TO THIS TREASURE TROVE OF...
SPLAT!
SLIME?
THESE POOR BOOKS HAVE BEEN DOWN HERE FOR 500 YEARS! THEY'VE BECOME A BIT MILDEWED!
WHAT AN IGNOBLE FATE FOR THE GREAT LIBRARY... TURNED TO GOO!
I COULD CRY ...IF I DIDN'T FEEL MORE LIKE DOING SOMETHING ELSE!
BUT DIDN'T THE ABBOT SAY SOMETHING ABOUT PRINTING COPIES!
YOU'RE RIGHT! C'MON... MAYBE HE'LL SEE US AGAIN!
PHEW! I WOULDN'T IF I WERE HIM!

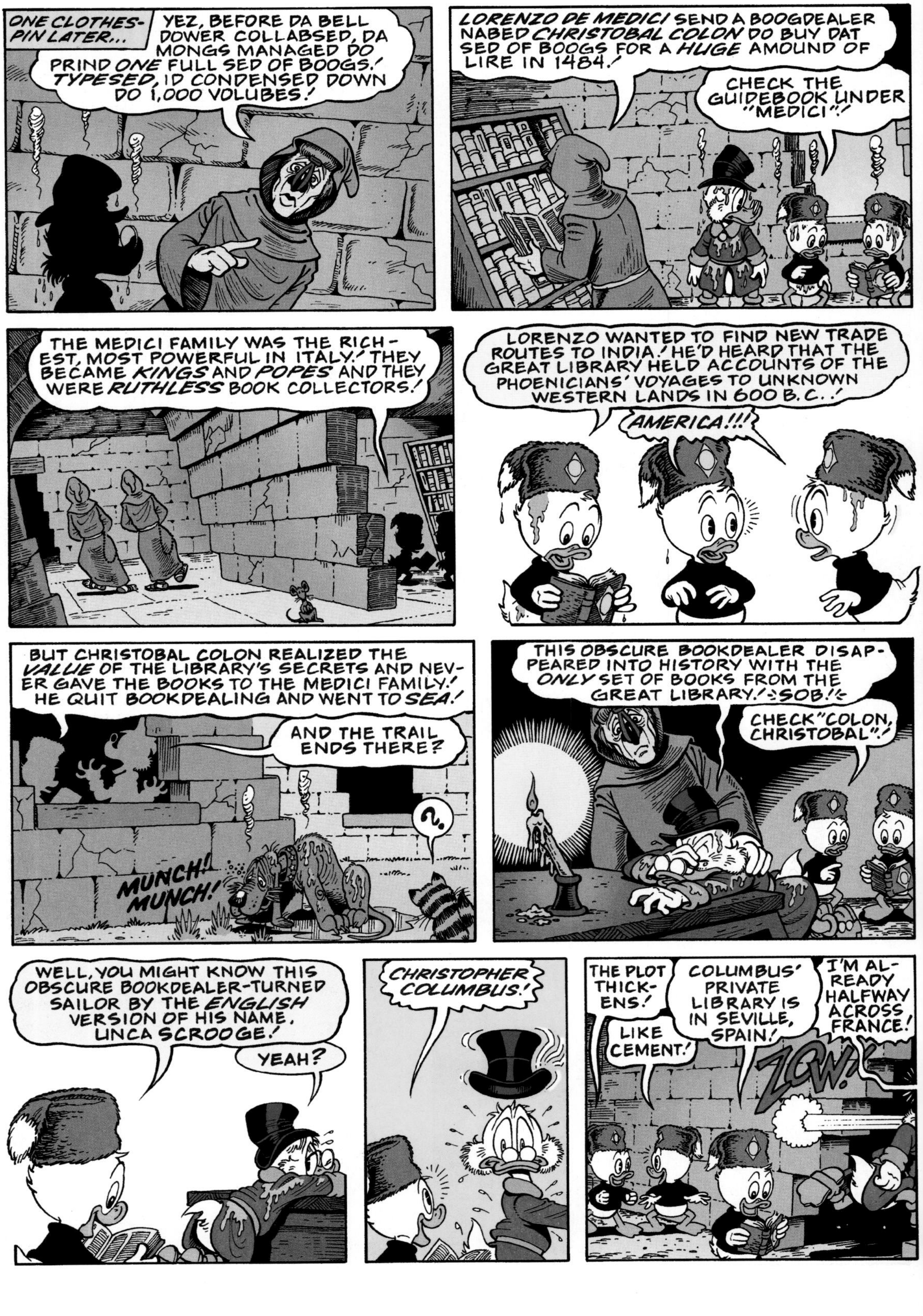
ONE CLOTHES-PIN LATER...
YEZ, BEFORE DA BELL DOWER COLLABSED, DA MONGS MANAGED DO PRIND ONE FULL SED OF BOOGS! TYPESED, ID CONDENSED DOWN DO 1,000 VOLUBES!
LORENZO DE MEDICI SEND A BOOGDEALER NABED CHRISTOBAL COLON DO BUY DAT SED OF BOOGS FOR A HUGE AMOUND OF LIRE IN 1484!
CHECK THE GUIDEBOOK UNDER "MEDICI"!
THE MEDICI FAMILY WAS THE RICH-EST, MOST POWERFUL IN ITALY! THEY BECAME KINGS AND POPES AND THEY WERE RUTHLESS BOOK COLLECTORS!
LORENZO WANTED TO FIND NEW TRADE ROUTES TO INDIA! HE'D HEARD THAT THE GREAT LIBRARY HELD ACCOUNTS OF THE PHOENICIANS' VOYAGES TO UNKNOWN WESTERN LANDS IN 600 B.C.!
AMERICA!!!
BUT CHRISTOBAL COLON REALIZED THE VALUE OF THE LIBRARY'S SECRETS AND NEV-ER GAVE THE BOOKS TO THE MEDICI FAMILY! HE QUIT BOOKDEALING AND WENT TO SEA!
AND THE TRAIL ENDS THERE?
MUNCH! MUNCH!
?
THIS OBSCURE BOOKDEALER DISAP-PEARED INTO HISTORY WITH THE ONLY SET OF BOOKS FROM THE GREAT LIBRARY! SOB!
CHECK "COLON, CHRISTOBAL"!
WELL, YOU MIGHT KNOW THIS OBSCURE BOOKDEALER-TURNED SAILOR BY THE ENGLISH VERSION OF HIS NAME, UNCA SCROOGE!
YEAH?
CHRISTOPHER COLUMBUS!
THE PLOT THICK-ENS!
LIKE CEMENT!
COLUMBUS' PRIVATE LIBRARY IS IN SEVILLE, SPAIN!
I'M AL-READY HALFWAY ACROSS FRANCE!
ZOW!

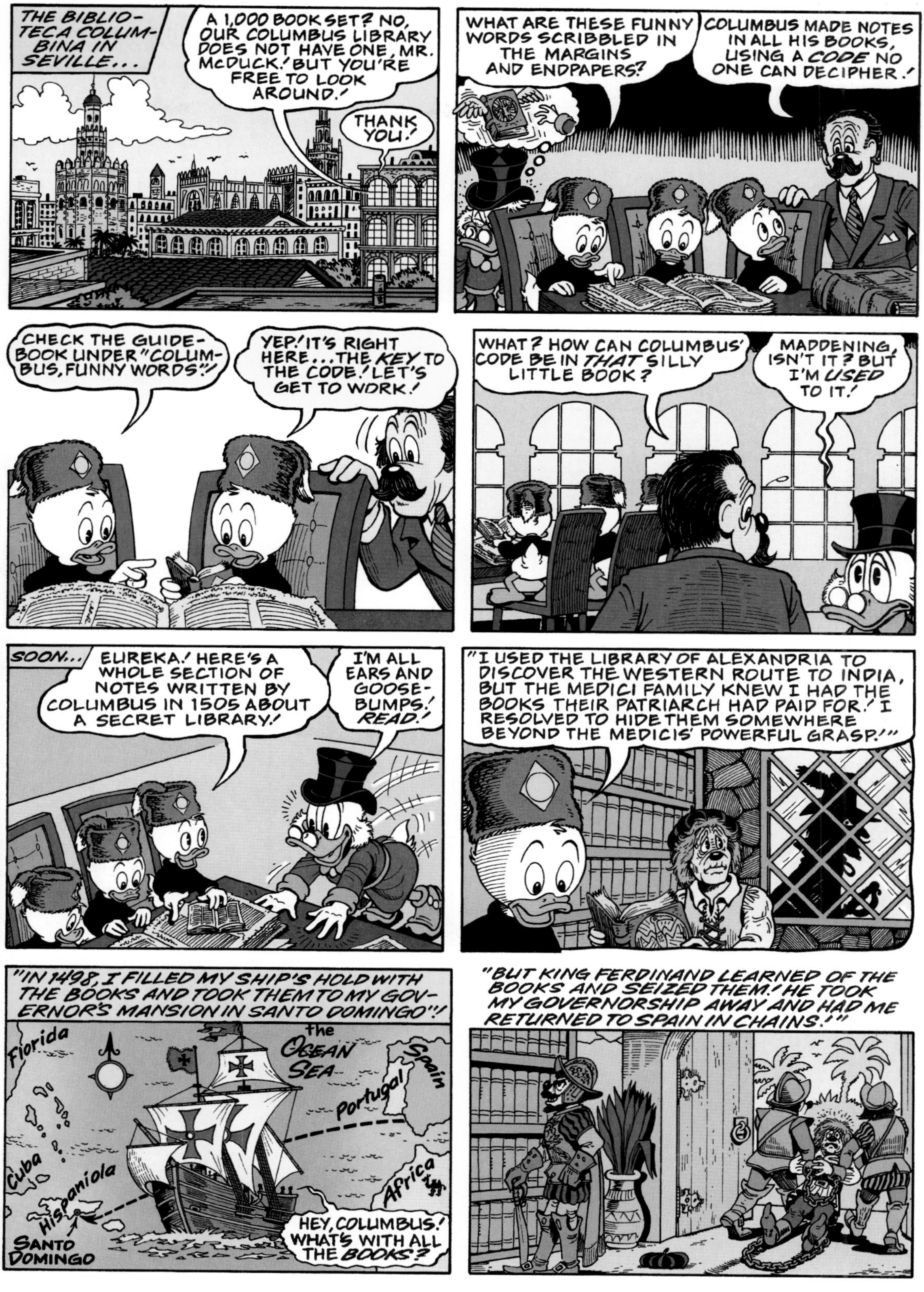
THE BIBLIOTECA COLUMBINA IN SEVILLE...
A 1,000 BOOK SET? NO, OUR COLUMBUS LIBRARY DOES NOT HAVE ONE, MR. McDUCK! BUT YOU'RE FREE TO LOOK AROUND!
THANK YOU!
WHAT ARE THESE FUNNY WORDS SCRIBBLED IN THE MARGINS AND ENDPAPERS?
COLUMBUS MADE NOTES IN ALL HIS BOOKS, USING A CODE NO ONE CAN DECIPHER!
CHECK THE GUIDEBOOK UNDER "COLUMBUS, FUNNY WORDS"!
YEP! IT'S RIGHT HERE... THE KEY TO THE CODE! LET'S GET TO WORK!
WHAT? HOW CAN COLUMBUS' CODE BE IN THAT SILLY LITTLE BOOK?
MADDENING, ISN'T IT? BUT I'M USED TO IT!
SOON...
EUREKA! HERE'S A WHOLE SECTION OF NOTES WRITTEN BY COLUMBUS IN 1505 ABOUT A SECRET LIBRARY!
I'M ALL EARS AND GOOSEBUMPS! READ!
"I USED THE LIBRARY OF ALEXANDRIA TO DISCOVER THE WESTERN ROUTE TO INDIA, BUT THE MEDICI FAMILY KNEW I HAD THE BOOKS THEIR PATRIARCH HAD PAID FOR! I RESOLVED TO HIDE THEM SOMEWHERE BEYOND THE MEDICIS' POWERFUL GRASP!"
"IN 1498, I FILLED MY SHIP'S HOLD WITH THE BOOKS AND TOOK THEM TO MY GOVERNOR'S MANSION IN SANTO DOMINGO"!
Florida
the OCEAN SEA
Spain
Portugal
Cuba
Hispaniola
Africa
SANTO DOMINGO
HEY, COLUMBUS! WHAT'S WITH ALL THE BOOKS?
"BUT KING FERDINAND LEARNED OF THE BOOKS AND SEIZED THEM! HE TOOK MY GOVERNORSHIP AWAY AND HAD ME RETURNED TO SPAIN IN CHAINS!"

"SOMEDAY I HOPE TO RECLAIM THE BOOKS AND USE THEM TO FIND THE LOST GOLD OF OPHIR, KING SOLOMON'S MINES, AND SO MUCH MORE!"

BUT COLUMBUS NEVER SAILED TO THE NEW WORLD AGAIN, AND HE DIED IN *POVERTY!*

SOUNDS LIKE YOU AND COLUMBUS ARE TREASURE-HUNTING BIRDS OF A FEATHER, UNCA SCROOGE!

MAYBE HE WAS PART SCOTTISH!

COULD THE LOST LIBRARY STILL BE IN THE WEST INDIES?

IF THEY EVER MOVED IT, IT WOULD BE MENTIONED IN THE LOGS OF THE SPANISH FLEET!

AND I *BOUGHT* THOSE RECORDS FOR USE IN SALVAGING TREASURE, REMEMBER?

BACK TO DUCK-BURG! WOW! THIS IS THE *BEST* TREASURE HUNT *EVER!*

*S*O THE MCDUCK/WOODCHUCK EXPED-ITION COMES FULL CIRCLE! WITHIN A DAY THEY ARE MARCHING UP KILL-MOTOR HILL TO THE MONEY BIN...

HANDS OFF!

SALESMEN ABANDON ALL HOPE!

HALT! WHO GOES THERE? PASS!

SOME *GUARD!* I COULD BE MAGICA DeSPELL TAKING THE BEAGLE BOYS ON A TOUR!

POW! BANG! KPOW!

WE'RE BACK, UNCA DONALD, AND WE'RE STILL ON THE TRAIL OF THE LOST LIBRARY! COME AND JOIN US!

HM...YEAH ...IN A MINUTE...

RIGHT NOW I'M WATCHING "GUNSMOG"! MATT SAVAGE IS IN A HIGH-SPEED KNIFE FIGHT WITH SOME CROOKS AND HIS HORSE JUST FLIPPED AND BURST INTO FLAMES!

POW! BLAM! QW!

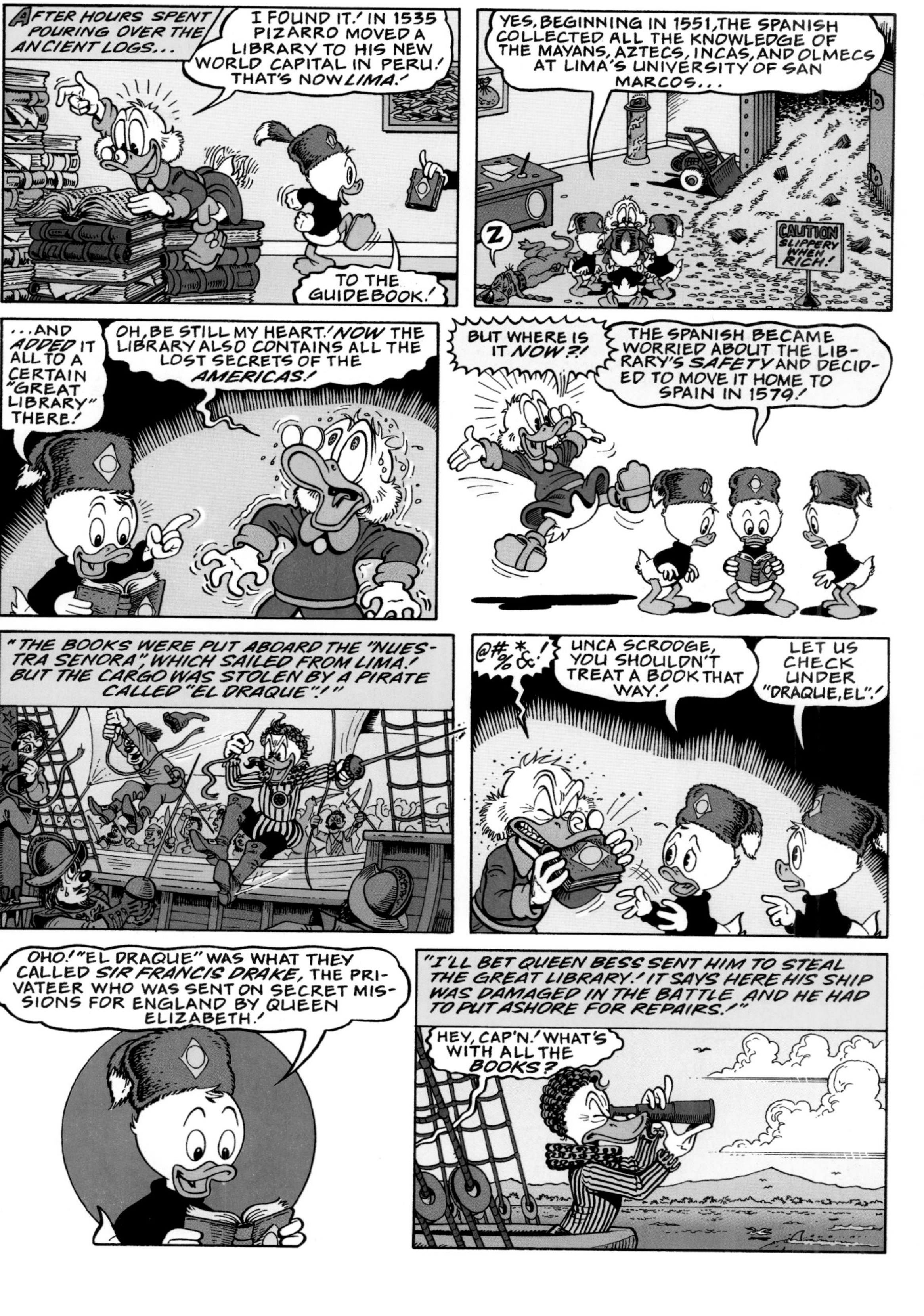
AFTER HOURS SPENT POURING OVER THE ANCIENT LOGS...
I FOUND IT! IN 1535 PIZARRO MOVED A LIBRARY TO HIS NEW WORLD CAPITAL IN PERU! THAT'S NOW LIMA!
TO THE GUIDEBOOK!
YES, BEGINNING IN 1551, THE SPANISH COLLECTED ALL THE KNOWLEDGE OF THE MAYANS, AZTECS, INCAS, AND OLMECS AT LIMA'S UNIVERSITY OF SAN MARCOS...
Z
CAUTION SLIPPERY WHEN RICH!
...AND ADDED IT ALL TO A CERTAIN "GREAT LIBRARY" THERE!
OH, BE STILL MY HEART! NOW THE LIBRARY ALSO CONTAINS ALL THE LOST SECRETS OF THE AMERICAS!
BUT WHERE IS IT NOW?!
THE SPANISH BECAME WORRIED ABOUT THE LIBRARY'S SAFETY AND DECIDED TO MOVE IT HOME TO SPAIN IN 1579!
"THE BOOKS WERE PUT ABOARD THE "NUESTRA SENORA", WHICH SAILED FROM LIMA! BUT THE CARGO WAS STOLEN BY A PIRATE CALLED "EL DRAQUE"!"
@#*%&!
UNCA SCROOGE, YOU SHOULDN'T TREAT A BOOK THAT WAY!
LET US CHECK UNDER "DRAQUE, EL"!
OHO! "EL DRAQUE" WAS WHAT THEY CALLED SIR FRANCIS DRAKE, THE PRIVATEER WHO WAS SENT ON SECRET MISSIONS FOR ENGLAND BY QUEEN ELIZABETH!
"I'LL BET QUEEN BESS SENT HIM TO STEAL THE GREAT LIBRARY! IT SAYS HERE HIS SHIP WAS DAMAGED IN THE BATTLE AND HE HAD TO PUT ASHORE FOR REPAIRS!"
HEY, CAP'N! WHAT'S WITH ALL THE BOOKS?

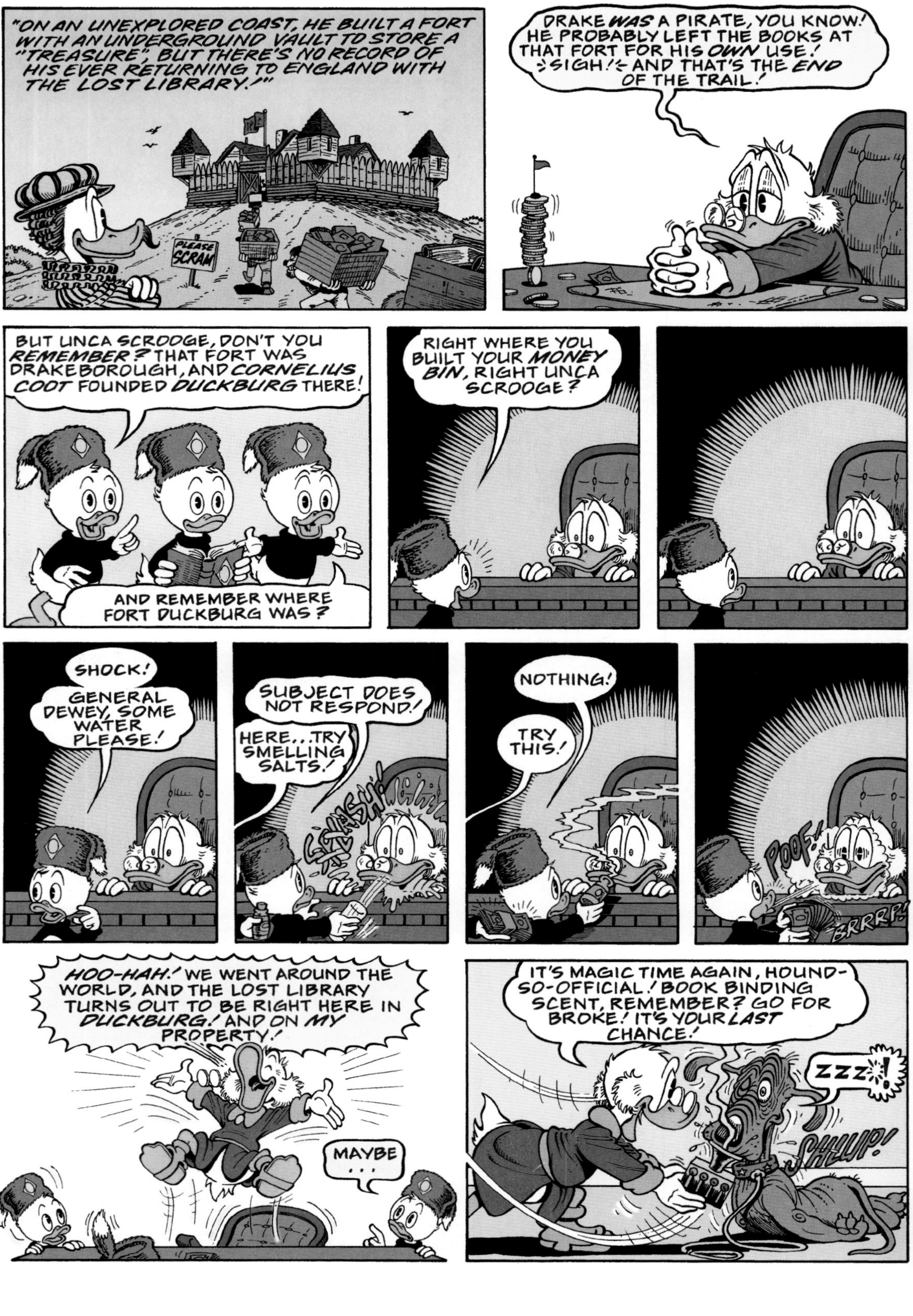
"ON AN UNEXPLORED COAST, HE BUILT A FORT WITH AN UNDERGROUND VAULT TO STORE A "TREASURE", BUT THERE'S NO RECORD OF HIS EVER RETURNING TO ENGLAND WITH THE LOST LIBRARY!'"
PLEASE SCRAM
DRAKE WAS A PIRATE, YOU KNOW! HE PROBABLY LEFT THE BOOKS AT THAT FORT FOR HIS OWN USE! SIGH! AND THAT'S THE END OF THE TRAIL!
BUT UNCA SCROOGE, DON'T YOU REMEMBER? THAT FORT WAS DRAKEBOROUGH, AND CORNELIUS COOT FOUNDED DUCKBURG THERE!
AND REMEMBER WHERE FORT DUCKBURG WAS?
RIGHT WHERE YOU BUILT YOUR MONEY BIN, RIGHT UNCA SCROOGE?
SHOCK!
GENERAL DEWEY, SOME WATER PLEASE!
SUBJECT DOES NOT RESPOND!
HERE...TRY SMELLING SALTS!
SPLASH!
NOTHING!
TRY THIS!
POOF!
BRRRP!
HOO-HAH! WE WENT AROUND THE WORLD, AND THE LOST LIBRARY TURNS OUT TO BE RIGHT HERE IN DUCKBURG! AND ON MY PROPERTY!
MAYBE . . .
IT'S MAGIC TIME AGAIN, HOUND-SO-OFFICIAL! BOOK BINDING SCENT, REMEMBER? GO FOR BROKE! IT'S YOUR LAST CHANCE!
ZZZ!
SHLUP!

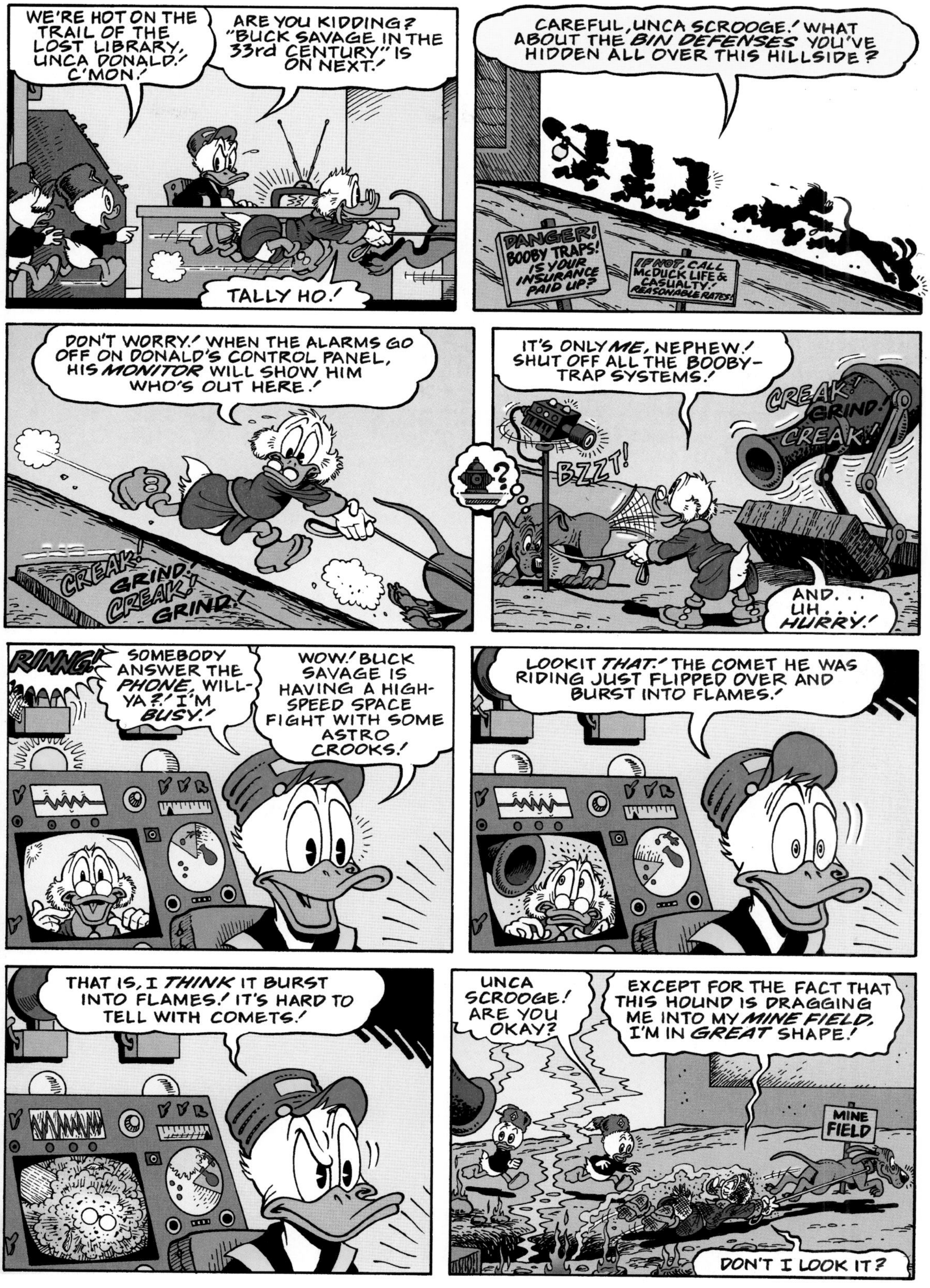
WE'RE HOT ON THE TRAIL OF THE LOST LIBRARY, UNCA DONALD! C'MON!
ARE YOU KIDDING? "BUCK SAVAGE IN THE 33rd CENTURY" IS ON NEXT!
TALLY HO!
CAREFUL, UNCA SCROOGE! WHAT ABOUT THE BIN DEFENSES YOU'VE HIDDEN ALL OVER THIS HILLSIDE?
DANGER! BOOBY TRAPS! IS YOUR INSURANCE PAID UP?
IF NOT, CALL McDUCK LIFE & CASUALTY! REASONABLE RATES!
DON'T WORRY! WHEN THE ALARMS GO OFF ON DONALD'S CONTROL PANEL, HIS MONITOR WILL SHOW HIM WHO'S OUT HERE!
CREAK! GRIND! CREAK! GRIND!
IT'S ONLY ME, NEPHEW! SHUT OFF ALL THE BOOBY-TRAP SYSTEMS!
CREAK! GRIND! CREAK!
BZZT!
AND... UH... HURRY!
RINNG!
SOMEBODY ANSWER THE PHONE, WILL-YA?! I'M BUSY!
WOW! BUCK SAVAGE IS HAVING A HIGH-SPEED SPACE FIGHT WITH SOME ASTRO CROOKS!
LOOKIT THAT! THE COMET HE WAS RIDING JUST FLIPPED OVER AND BURST INTO FLAMES!
THAT IS, I THINK IT BURST INTO FLAMES! IT'S HARD TO TELL WITH COMETS!
UNCA SCROOGE! ARE YOU OKAY?
EXCEPT FOR THE FACT THAT THIS HOUND IS DRAGGING ME INTO MY MINE FIELD, I'M IN GREAT SHAPE!
MINE FIELD
DON'T I LOOK IT?

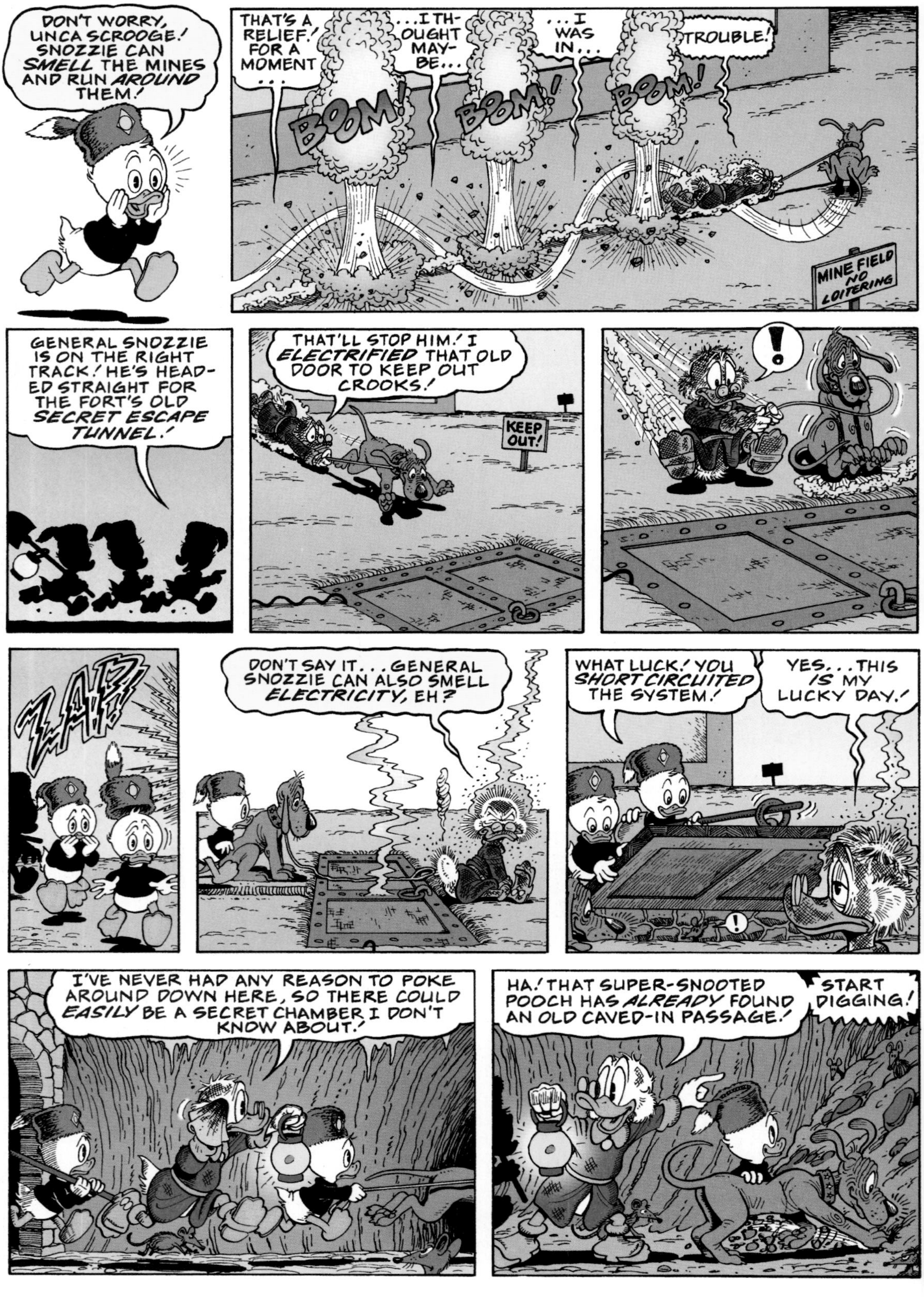

DON'T WORRY, UNCA SCROOGE! SNOZZIE CAN SMELL THE MINES AND RUN AROUND THEM!
THAT'S A RELIEF! FOR A MOMENT . . .
. . . I TH-OUGHT MAY-BE . . .
. . . I WAS IN . . .
TROUBLE!
BOOM!
BOOM!
BOOM!
MINE FIELD NO LOITERING
GENERAL SNOZZIE IS ON THE RIGHT TRACK! HE'S HEAD-ED STRAIGHT FOR THE FORT'S OLD SECRET ESCAPE TUNNEL!
THAT'LL STOP HIM! I ELECTRIFIED THAT OLD DOOR TO KEEP OUT CROOKS!
KEEP OUT!
!
ZAP!
DON'T SAY IT . . . GENERAL SNOZZIE CAN ALSO SMELL ELECTRICITY, EH?
WHAT LUCK! YOU SHORT CIRCUITED THE SYSTEM!
YES . . . THIS IS MY LUCKY DAY!
!
I'VE NEVER HAD ANY REASON TO POKE AROUND DOWN HERE, SO THERE COULD EASILY BE A SECRET CHAMBER I DON'T KNOW ABOUT!
HA! THAT SUPER-SNOOTED POOCH HAS ALREADY FOUND AN OLD CAVED-IN PASSAGE!
START DIGGING!

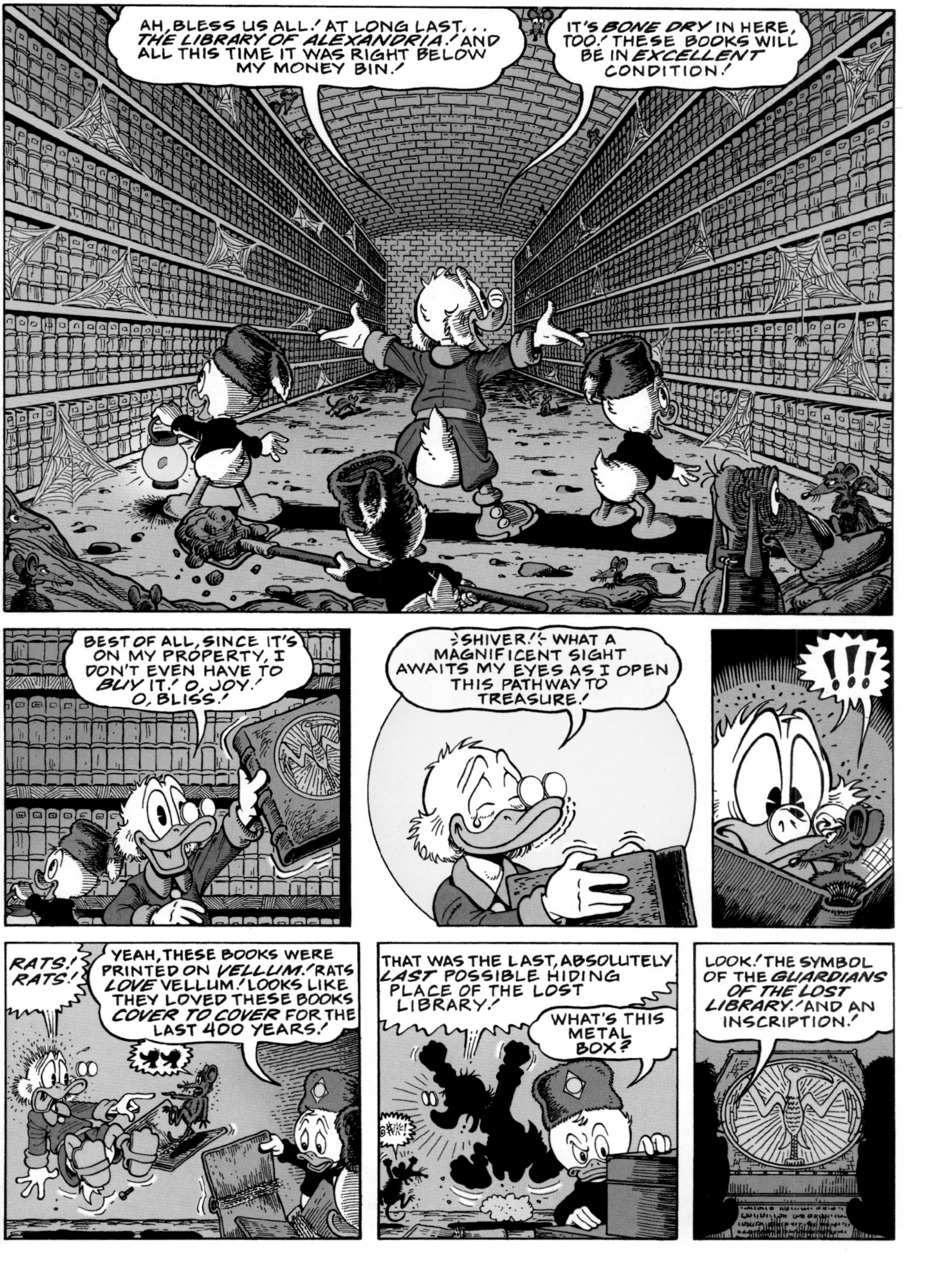
AH, BLESS US ALL! AT LONG LAST... THE LIBRARY OF ALEXANDRIA! AND ALL THIS TIME IT WAS RIGHT BELOW MY MONEY BIN!
IT'S BONE DRY IN HERE, TOO! THESE BOOKS WILL BE IN EXCELLENT CONDITION!
BEST OF ALL, SINCE IT'S ON MY PROPERTY, I DON'T EVEN HAVE TO BUY IT! O, JOY! O, BLISS!
SHIVER! WHAT A MAGNIFICENT SIGHT AWAITS MY EYES AS I OPEN THIS PATHWAY TO TREASURE!
!!!
RATS! RATS!
YEAH, THESE BOOKS WERE PRINTED ON VELLUM! RATS LOVE VELLUM! LOOKS LIKE THEY LOVED THESE BOOKS COVER TO COVER FOR THE LAST 400 YEARS!
THAT WAS THE LAST, ABSOLUTELY LAST POSSIBLE HIDING PLACE OF THE LOST LIBRARY!
WHAT'S THIS METAL BOX?
LOOK! THE SYMBOL OF THE GUARDIANS OF THE LOST LIBRARY! AND AN INSCRIPTION!

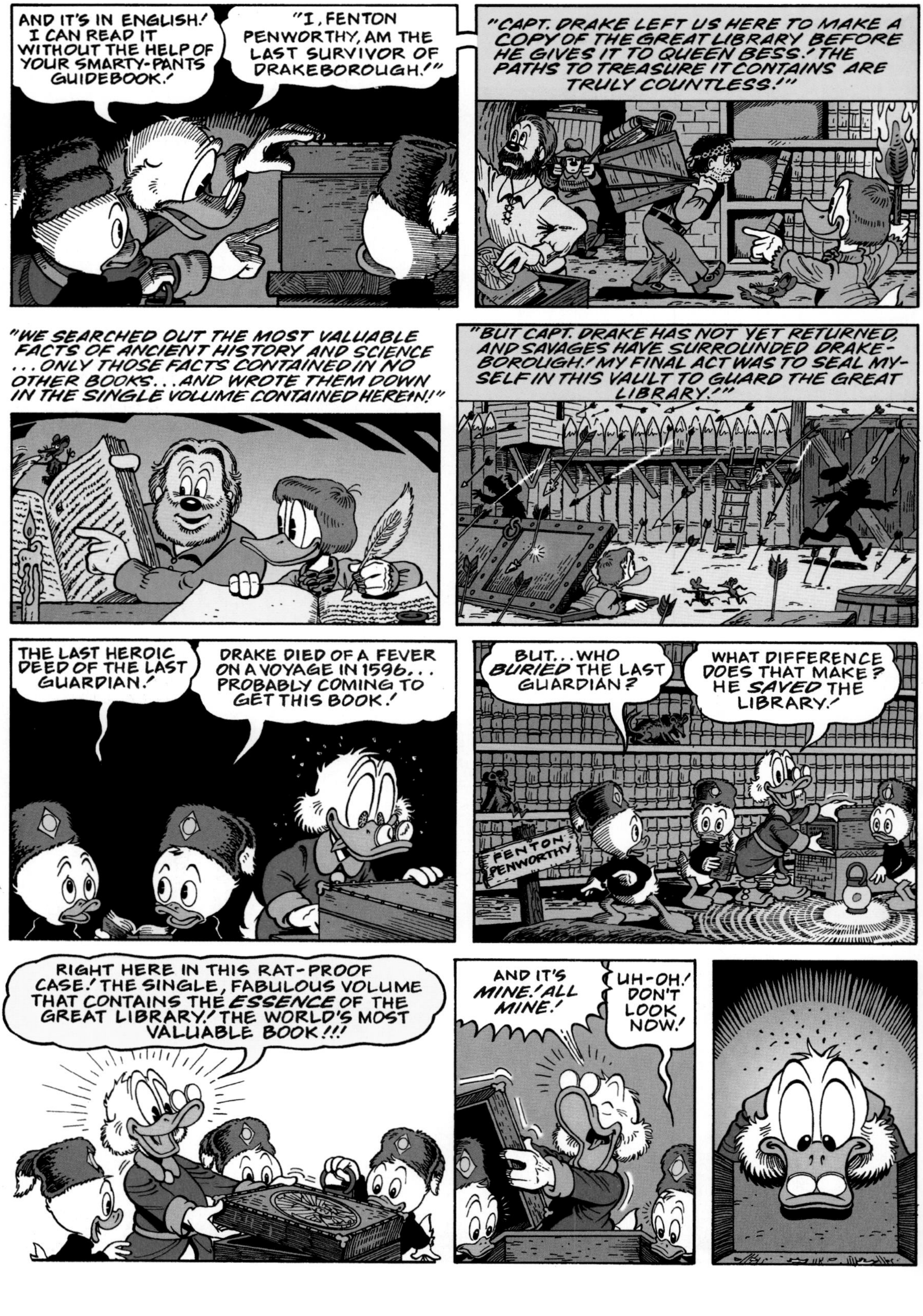

AND IT'S IN ENGLISH! I CAN READ IT WITHOUT THE HELP OF YOUR SMARTY-PANTS GUIDEBOOK!
"I, FENTON PENWORTHY, AM THE LAST SURVIVOR OF DRAKEBOROUGH!"
"CAPT. DRAKE LEFT US HERE TO MAKE A COPY OF THE GREAT LIBRARY BEFORE HE GIVES IT TO QUEEN BESS! THE PATHS TO TREASURE IT CONTAINS ARE TRULY COUNTLESS!"
"WE SEARCHED OUT THE MOST VALUABLE FACTS OF ANCIENT HISTORY AND SCIENCE . . . ONLY THOSE FACTS CONTAINED IN NO OTHER BOOKS . . . AND WROTE THEM DOWN IN THE SINGLE VOLUME CONTAINED HEREIN!"
"BUT CAPT. DRAKE HAS NOT YET RETURNED, AND SAVAGES HAVE SURROUNDED DRAKEBOROUGH! MY FINAL ACT WAS TO SEAL MYSELF IN THIS VAULT TO GUARD THE GREAT LIBRARY!"
THE LAST HEROIC DEED OF THE LAST GUARDIAN!
DRAKE DIED OF A FEVER ON A VOYAGE IN 1596. . . PROBABLY COMING TO GET THIS BOOK!
BUT. . . WHO BURIED THE LAST GUARDIAN?
WHAT DIFFERENCE DOES THAT MAKE? HE SAVED THE LIBRARY!
FENTON PENWORTHY
RIGHT HERE IN THIS RAT-PROOF CASE! THE SINGLE, FABULOUS VOLUME THAT CONTAINS THE ESSENCE OF THE GREAT LIBRARY! THE WORLD'S MOST VALUABLE BOOK!!!
AND IT'S MINE! ALL MINE!
UH-OH! DON'T LOOK NOW!

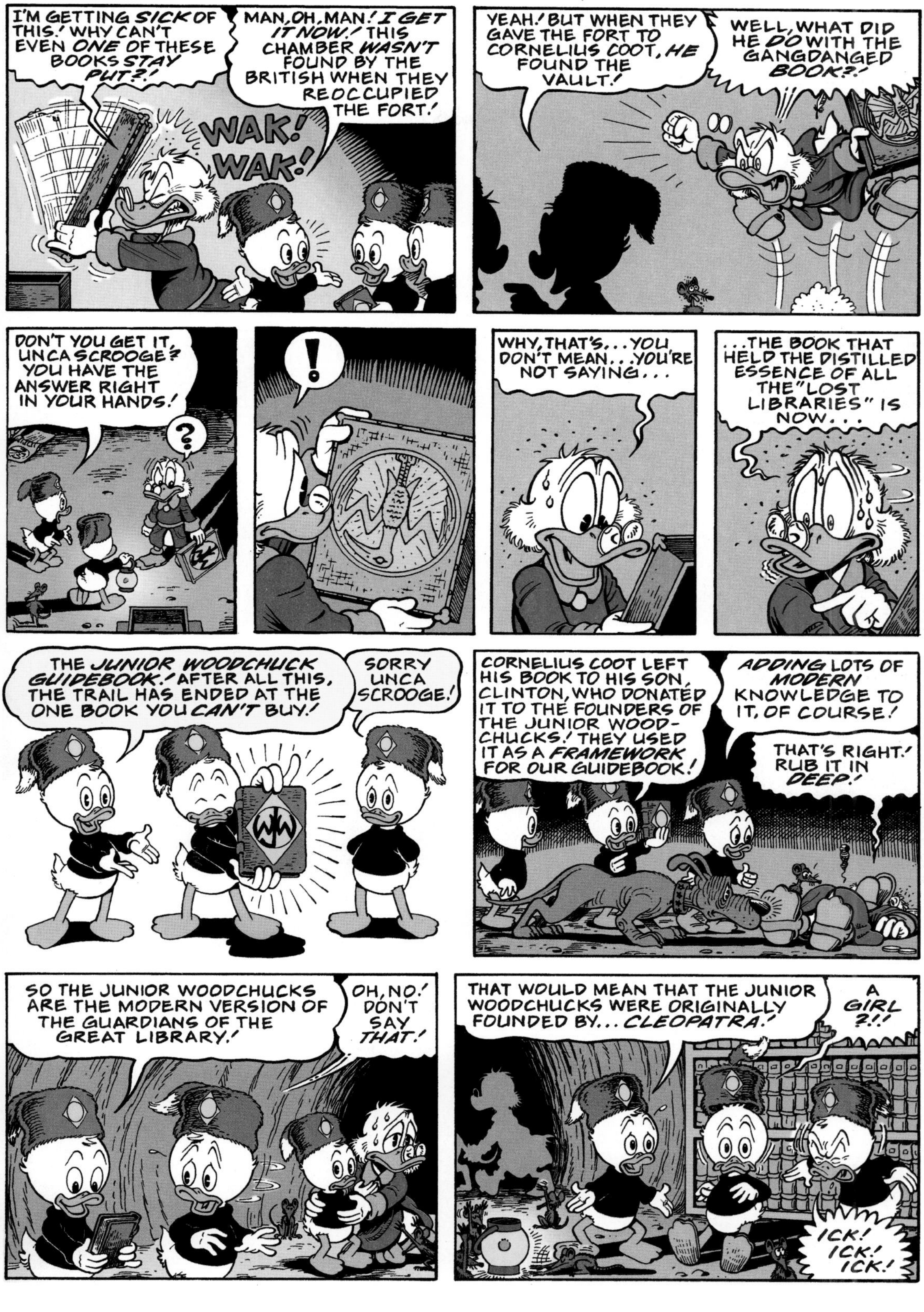
I'M GETTING SICK OF THIS! WHY CAN'T EVEN ONE OF THESE BOOKS STAY PUT?!
MAN, OH, MAN! I GET IT NOW! THIS CHAMBER WASN'T FOUND BY THE BRITISH WHEN THEY REOCCUPIED THE FORT!
WAK! WAK!
YEAH! BUT WHEN THEY GAVE THE FORT TO CORNELIUS COOT, HE FOUND THE VAULT!
WELL, WHAT DID HE DO WITH THE GANGDANGED BOOK?!
DON'T YOU GET IT, UNCA SCROOGE? YOU HAVE THE ANSWER RIGHT IN YOUR HANDS!
?
!
WHY, THAT'S... YOU DON'T MEAN... YOU'RE NOT SAYING...
...THE BOOK THAT HELD THE DISTILLED ESSENCE OF ALL THE "LOST LIBRARIES" IS NOW...
THE JUNIOR WOODCHUCK GUIDEBOOK! AFTER ALL THIS, THE TRAIL HAS ENDED AT THE ONE BOOK YOU CAN'T BUY!
SORRY UNCA SCROOGE!
CORNELIUS COOT LEFT HIS BOOK TO HIS SON, CLINTON, WHO DONATED IT TO THE FOUNDERS OF THE JUNIOR WOOD-CHUCKS! THEY USED IT AS A FRAMEWORK FOR OUR GUIDEBOOK!
ADDING LOTS OF MODERN KNOWLEDGE TO IT, OF COURSE!
THAT'S RIGHT! RUB IT IN DEEP!
SO THE JUNIOR WOODCHUCKS ARE THE MODERN VERSION OF THE GUARDIANS OF THE GREAT LIBRARY!
OH, NO! DON'T SAY THAT!
THAT WOULD MEAN THAT THE JUNIOR WOODCHUCKS WERE ORIGINALLY FOUNDED BY... CLEOPATRA!
A GIRL?!!
ICK! ICK! ICK!

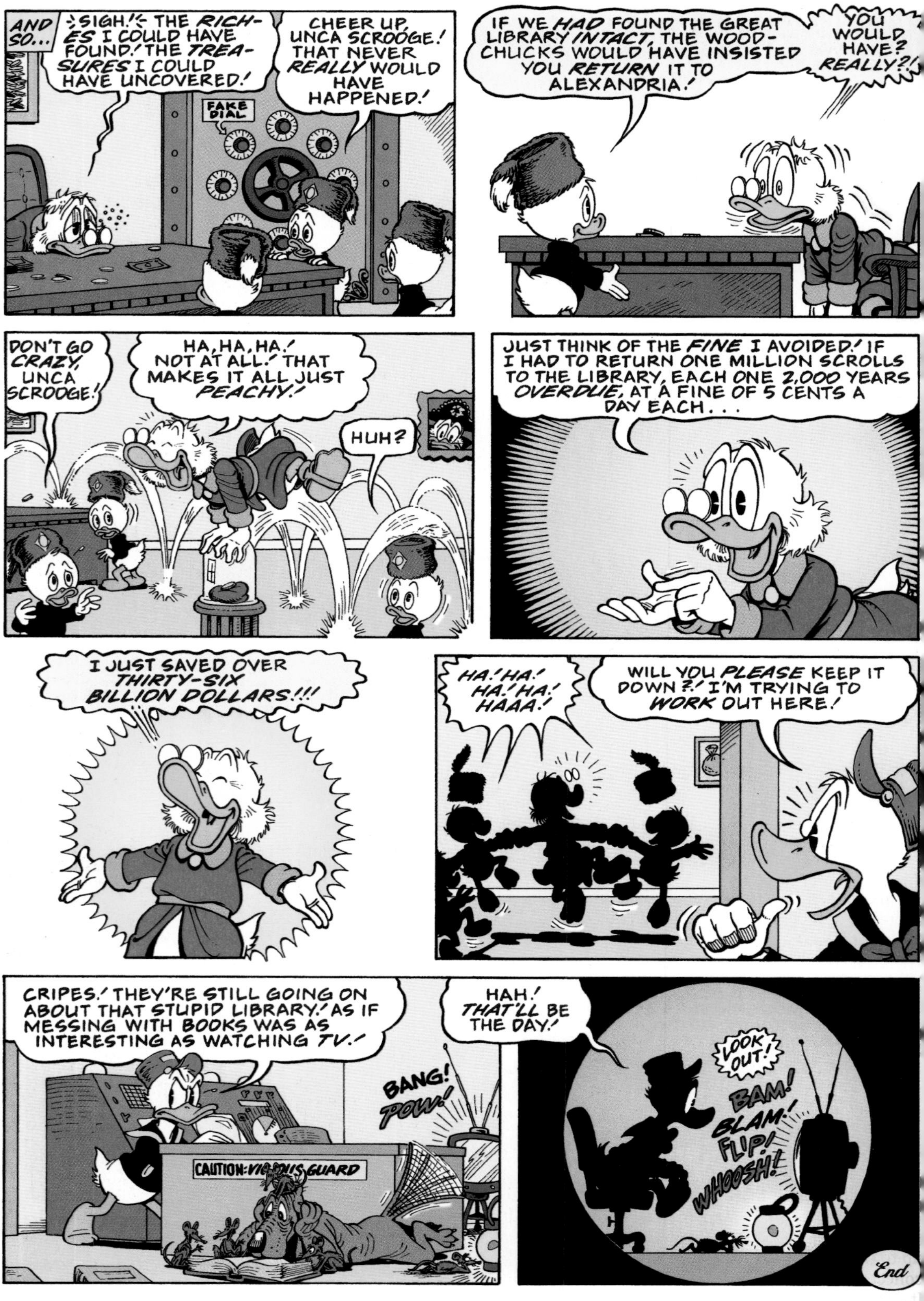
AND SO...
SIGH! THE RICHES I COULD HAVE FOUND! THE TREASURES I COULD HAVE UNCOVERED!
FAKE DIAL
CHEER UP, UNCA SCROOGE! THAT NEVER REALLY WOULD HAVE HAPPENED!
IF WE HAD FOUND THE GREAT LIBRARY INTACT, THE WOODCHUCKS WOULD HAVE INSISTED YOU RETURN IT TO ALEXANDRIA!
YOU WOULD HAVE? REALLY?!
DON'T GO CRAZY, UNCA SCROOGE!
HA, HA, HA! NOT AT ALL! THAT MAKES IT ALL JUST PEACHY!
HUH?
JUST THINK OF THE FINE I AVOIDED! IF I HAD TO RETURN ONE MILLION SCROLLS TO THE LIBRARY, EACH ONE 2,000 YEARS OVERDUE, AT A FINE OF 5 CENTS A DAY EACH . . .
I JUST SAVED OVER THIRTY-SIX BILLION DOLLARS!!!
HA! HA! HA! HA! HAAA!
WILL YOU PLEASE KEEP IT DOWN?! I'M TRYING TO WORK OUT HERE!
CRIPES! THEY'RE STILL GOING ON ABOUT THAT STUPID LIBRARY! AS IF MESSING WITH BOOKS WAS AS INTERESTING AS WATCHING TV!
BANG! POW!
HAH! THAT'LL BE THE DAY!
LOOK OUT!
BAM! BLAM! FLIP! WHOOSH!
End

GUARDIANS *of the* LOST LIBRARY

Commentary by Don Rosa

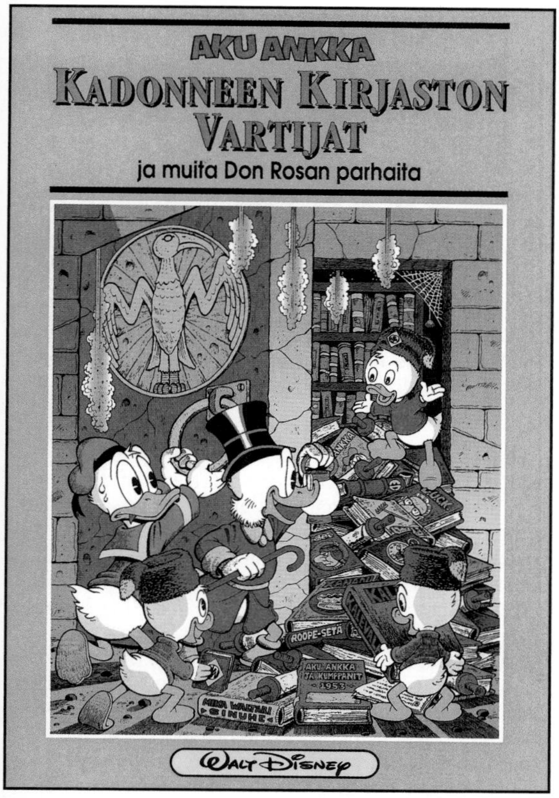
AKU ANKKA
KADONNEEN KIRJASTON VARTIJAT
ja muita Don Rosan parhaita
ROOPE-SETÄ
AKU ANKKA JA KUMPPANIT 1953
WALT DISNEY

Don Rosa's 1995 cover for a Finnish collected volume including "Guardians of the Lost Library" and other Duck stories. Wak! It looks like this screwy version of the Lost Library contains Finnish comic books featuring those other stories!

This is a significant story in my career for several reasons. First of all, it was done especially at the request of my good friends in Norway—in 1993, Norway was officially celebrating "The Year of the Book" to promote reading, and the Norwegian Egmont publisher, himself a scholar of classical literature, asked me to write a Duck adventure about books. This immediately suggested to me that it would be an excellent opportunity to send Scrooge McDuck on another epic quest, this time in search for the ancient Library of Alexandria.

What if the Library had not been lost to the world, but had been preserved over the centuries by a secret society? As I created a complex plot that would trace the Library through centuries of intrigue, I could show the evolution of books from papyrus scrolls through parchment tomes and the first Gutenberg volumes on up to the present day. I could mention actual famous collectors or dealers in books, such as—respectively—Italy's Medici clan and Christopher Columbus. In the process, it was easy to show how books have recorded and even inspired the advancements of science and art through the ages, particularly in bygone days when wealthy people measured their worth in how many books they owned. Along the way I even visit a modern newsstand with its contribution to the written realm of knowledge and entertainment (including comic books!). And what could be better than for the key to tracing the Library around the world be that most famous mythical book of all—the Junior Woodchuck Guidebook?!

I also put Donald to special use by taking him out of the main action for once, and making him an example of a modern TV zombie whose will to read has been corrupted by our limitless junk entertainment. As the typical "everyman" character, Donald filled that role well!

Another special attribute of this adventure was how similar it is to my more recent story about the treasure of the Knights Templar ("The Old Castle's Other Secret," *US* 342)—I thought I had lost control in my joy of research, and that I had packed too much info into "Guardians" and not enough action. However, like

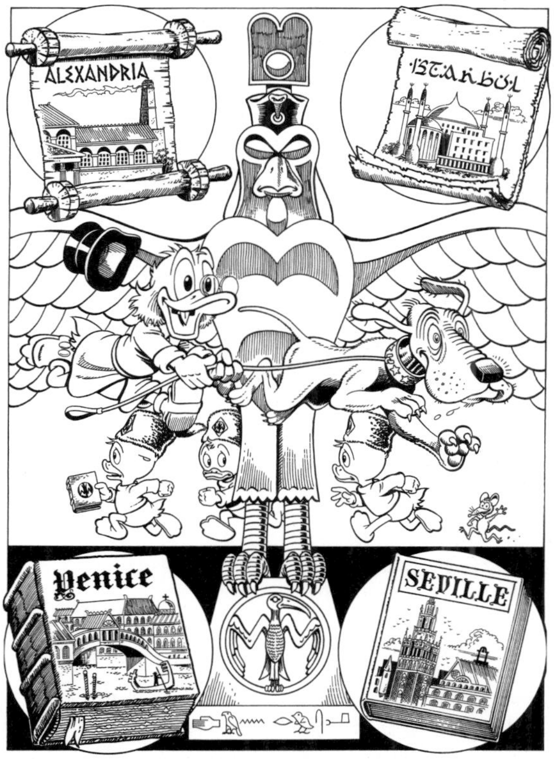
ALEXANDRIA
ISTANBUL
Venice
SEVILLE

Full version of this issue's cover image, as initially rendered for a poster in France's *Picsou* 385 (2004). The four corner insets feature lettering by Todd Klein—and the hieroglyphics at the statue's base phonetically say "dahn rowsuh" in ancient Egyptian!

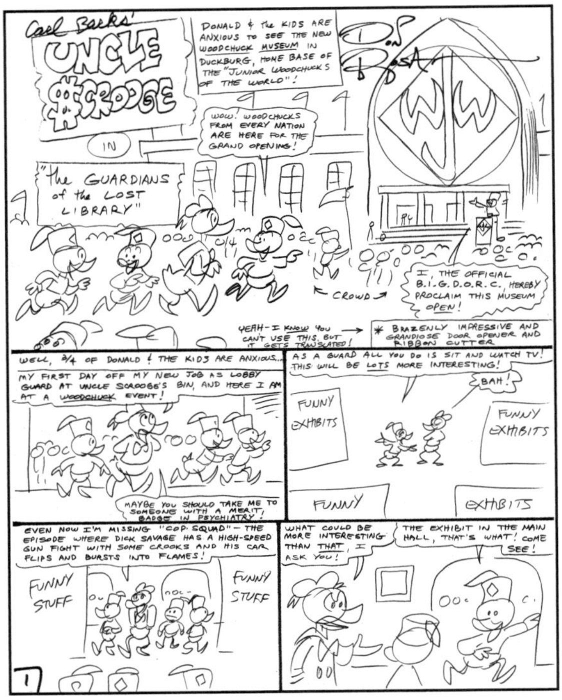
Carl Barks'
UNCLE $CROOGE
IN
"the GUARDIANS of the LOST LIBRARY"
DONALD & the KIDS ARE ANXIOUS TO SEE THE NEW WOODCHUCK MUSEUM IN DUCKBURG, HOME BASE OF THE "JUNIOR WOODCHUCKS OF THE WORLD"!
WOW! WOODCHUCKS FROM EVERY NATION ARE HERE FOR THE GRAND OPENING!
CROWD
I, THE OFFICIAL B.I.G.D.O.R.C., HEREBY PROCLAIM THIS MUSEUM OPEN!
YEAH—I KNOW YOU CAN'T USE THIS. BUT IT GETS TRANSLATED!
* BRAZENLY IMPRESSIVE AND GRANDIOSE DOOR OPENER AND RIBBON CUTTER
WELL, 3/4 OF DONALD & THE KIDS ARE ANXIOUS...
MY FIRST DAY OFF MY NEW JOB AS LOBBY GUARD AT UNCLE SCROOGE'S BIN, AND HERE I AM AT A WOODCHUCK EVENT!
MAYBE YOU SHOULD TAKE ME TO SOMEONE WITH A MERIT BADGE IN PSYCHIATRY!
AS A GUARD ALL YOU DO IS SIT AND WATCH TV! THIS WILL BE LOTS MORE INTERESTING!
BAH!
FUNNY EXHIBITS
FUNNY EXHIBITS
FUNNY
EXHIBITS
EVEN NOW I'M MISSING "COP SQUAD"—THE EPISODE WHERE DICK SAVAGE HAS A HIGH-SPEED GUN FIGHT WITH SOME CROOKS AND HIS CAR FLIPS AND BURSTS INTO FLAMES!
FUNNY STUFF
FUNNY STUFF
WHAT COULD BE MORE INTERESTING THAN THAT, I ASK YOU!
THE EXHIBIT IN THE MAIN HALL, THAT'S WHAT! COME SEE!
1

Page 1 of Don Rosa's original scribble-script for the "Guardians" story.

with my Templar treasure story, many readers did not agree with my self-criticism. "Guardians," more than any other I've ever done, has most often been referred to in mail I receive as "the best Rosa story" or "the best Duck story" or even "the best comic book story" (?!!) that fans say they've ever read. Well, I just hope new readers will at least regard it better than I did at the time!

But I so easily lose control during research. The most enjoyable part of constructing a Scrooge treasure hunt like this one is the challenge of making sure that every bit of history in my story is absolutely authentic. With weeks of research (using books!) I made certain that every name, date, place and event I utilized was true. Even though it's sometimes frustrating to know that many readers think I make all this stuff up out of my imagination, at least I know that when my story claims that, for example, Sir Francis Drake plundered a certain Spanish treasure ship sailing from a certain port on a certain date, it's all absolutely authentic. And that makes it fun for me!

Speaking of Drake, the scene where I have him establishing a lost British fort on the west coast of North America is also a fact, and though most historians think it was near present-day San Francisco, I moved it north a bit and decided it was on the site of Duckburg. This was a "fact" I established in a story several years earlier titled "His Majesty McDuck," last reprinted in *Uncle Scrooge* 331 (2004).

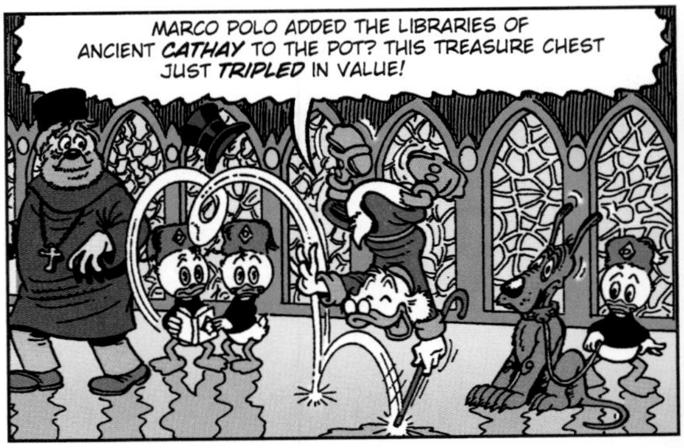
MARCO POLO ADDED THE LIBRARIES OF ANCIENT CATHAY TO THE POT? THIS TREASURE CHEST JUST TRIPLED IN VALUE!

The deleted panel from Don's original version of "Guardians." In the restaged replacement version, Scrooge has his giddy fit in the Abbey of San Slanti instead.

Though I try to be careful and keep my notes orderly, I juggled so many facts, names, and dates in "Guardians" that I made an error that was reported to me by a reader after the original publication in Europe—I had Marco Polo visit the library in Constantinople 50 years before he was born! For the first American edition I corrected this, adding several new panels of story and art to the Venice portion of the story that told of Mr. Polo's link with the Library occurring more appropriately during his lifetime. This meant the deletion of one panel from the original Istanbul (Constantinople) sequence and a shifting of other panels to fill various gaps. Note how one of the resulting pages features two full-page-wide panels in a row—normally I would never do that. That second wide panel had previously appeared at the top of the next page. The original deleted panel is reprinted here for your amusement.

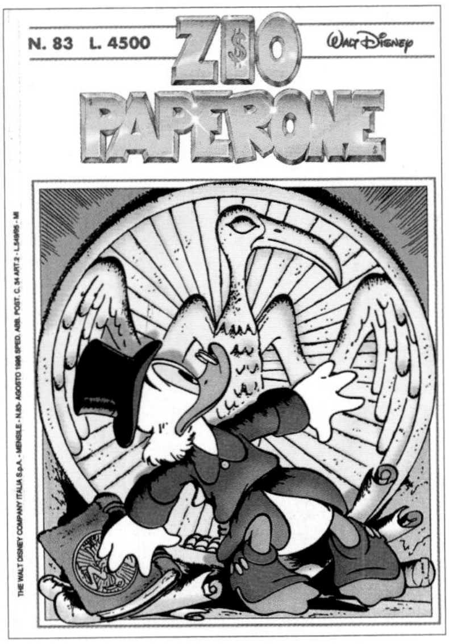
N. 83 L. 4500
ZIO PAPERONE
Walt Disney

Aside from the slight matter of having Marco Polo doing something before he existed, the only other part of this adventure that is part of my imagination is how the lost Library of Alexandria is intertwined throughout these historical events and personalities. Well, perhaps I also made up the Abbey of San Slanti in Venice. And there may not really be a place called Duckburg... except in our hearts.

Don Rosa isn't the only Duck creator to have visited the Lost Library. This splendid Marco Rota cover decorated the story's Italian printing in *Zio Paperone* 83 (1996).

GUARDIAN *of the* LOST JUNIOR WOODCHUCK EMBLEM

Commentary by Don Rosa

That's me!

In "Guardians" there is one link between the ancient secret society of the Guardians of the Library of Alexandria, founded by Cleopatra VII, and the Junior Woodchucks of the World, founded by Clinton Coot of Duckburg. That link is their sacred emblem!

As we know, Carl Barks created an emblem for his wonderful "Junior Woodchucks of the World" which contained those initials of J.W.W. But since the Woodchucks have different names in the translations of Barks' stories in all other countries, this emblem could never be used in anything but the American editions.

When I write a Duck story, I know that very few Americans will see it, compared to the untold millions of Barks/Duck fans who will see it in Europe and South America and Asia. And yet, I am an American writing in America and I cannot avoid getting ideas that would make sense only for American Duck fans like myself. In those cases, I file the idea away and sometimes am able to add it later to the American printing of the story.

In this instance, my bright idea involved Barks' Junior Woodchucks emblem. While I was researching the history of books, I discovered that the first Guardians in my story, the Egyptians, regarded the god Thoth, represented by an ibis bird, to be the creator and symbol of written knowledge. Books. As I studied the Egyptian Thoth symbol, something crept into my mind... the bird's long curved beak... the upheld wings... what did that remind me of...? Then I happened to look at the Thoth symbol upside-down—yoicks! It was Barks' Junior Woodchucks of the World symbol!!! The ibis' thin body and curved beak profile made the central "J", and the two wings and forked tail halves made the two flanking "W"s!!! And my story involved the Woodchucks as being the modern successors of the Egyptian Guardians! Sometimes these ideas from history books are so good it's scary! But this particular idea only made sense in America. So my script contained some panels of dialogue that would be deleted from the Egmont version of the story and used only in American printings. Art differed, too. The Egmont version had Woodchuck emblems removed throughout the story and one panel widened, as seen here: the panel before Scrooge discovers the symbol similarity was extended to replace the American panel showing the discovery.

DON'T YOU GET IT, UNCA SCROOGE? CORNELIUS COOT LEFT HIS BOOK TO HIS SON, CLINTON, WHO DONATED IT TO THE FOUNDERS OF THE JUNIOR WOODCHUCKS!
AND GUESS WHAT *THEY* DID WITH IT!
?

Don's wider Egmont version of a panel from page 27. Note the different dialogue—moved from elsewhere on the page to cover over the Woodchuck symbol's absence.

Gladstone
Walt Disney's
27 $1.50 JULY $2.00 CANADIAN
UNCLE $CROOGE ADVENTURES

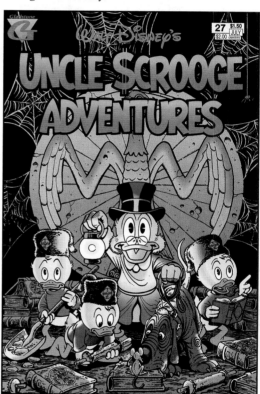

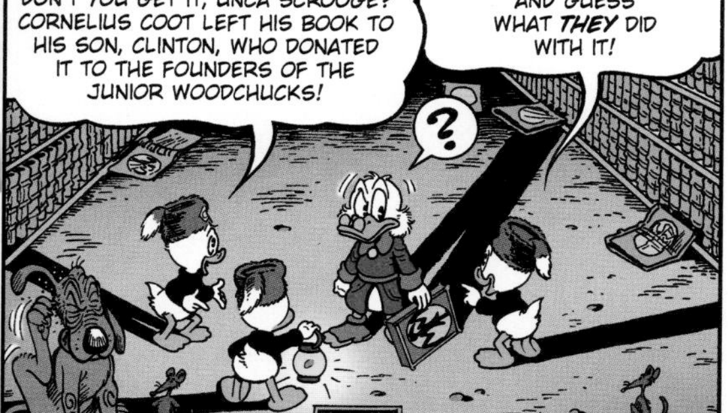

The original American cover for "Guardians of the Lost Library" (*Uncle Scrooge Adventures* 27, 1994).

The symbol similarity also comes into play on the original American cover for the story (*Uncle Scrooge Adventures* 27). My idea was that after a reader finished the story and closed the comic, he'd see the Guardian emblem and Woodchuck emblems there for easy comparison, and realize that a clue to the surprise ending of the story was right on the cover! Unfortunately, Egmont editors went a bit too far on their versions of the cover—they added text blurbs revealing to readers that this was "the origin story behind the Junior Woodchucks Guidebook," revealing the surprise ending of the story a little too completely! This is one of those reasons my hair is now gray. Or gone.

CHRISTMAS PARADE 5

December 2008

© 2008 Disney Enterprises, Inc.

A NEW COLLECTION OF HOLIDAY TALES

THE THRIFTY SPENDTHRIFT
Story and art by Carl Barks

MEMOIRS OF AN INVISIBLE SANTA
Story by Guido Martina, art by Romano Scarpa

COOKERY COUNTDOWN
Story by Pat & Shelly Block, art by Tino Santanach

'TIS BETTER TO GIVE THAN TO DECEIVE
Story by Stefan Petrucha, art by José Ramón Bernadó

MR. CLERKLY'S CHRISTMAS
Story and art by Kari Korhonen

On sale now at your favorite comic book store. Ask for it or visit
www.gemstonepub.com/disney.

Walt Disney's

The Jr Woodchucks -in- Gloom of the Unknown Author

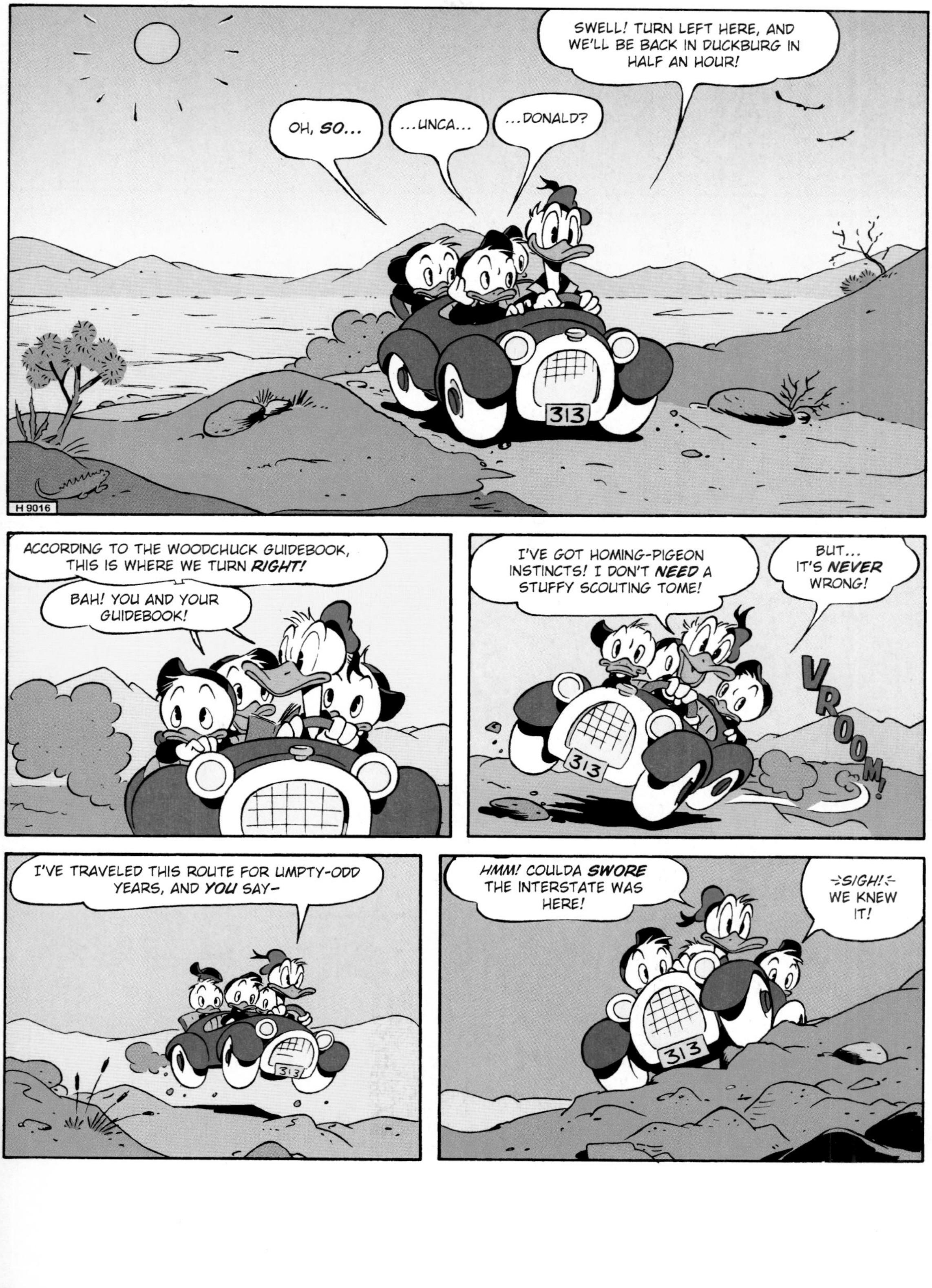

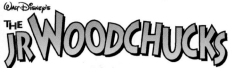

SWELL! TURN LEFT HERE, AND WE'LL BE BACK IN DUCKBURG IN HALF AN HOUR!
OH, *SO...*
...UNCA...
...DONALD?
H 9016
ACCORDING TO THE WOODCHUCK GUIDEBOOK, THIS IS WHERE WE TURN *RIGHT!*
BAH! YOU AND YOUR GUIDEBOOK!
I'VE GOT HOMING-PIGEON INSTINCTS! I DON'T *NEED* A STUFFY SCOUTING TOME!
BUT... IT'S *NEVER* WRONG!
VROOOM!
I'VE TRAVELED THIS ROUTE FOR UMPTY-ODD YEARS, AND *YOU* SAY–
HMM! COULDA *SWORE* THE INTERSTATE WAS HERE!
SIGH! WE KNEW IT!

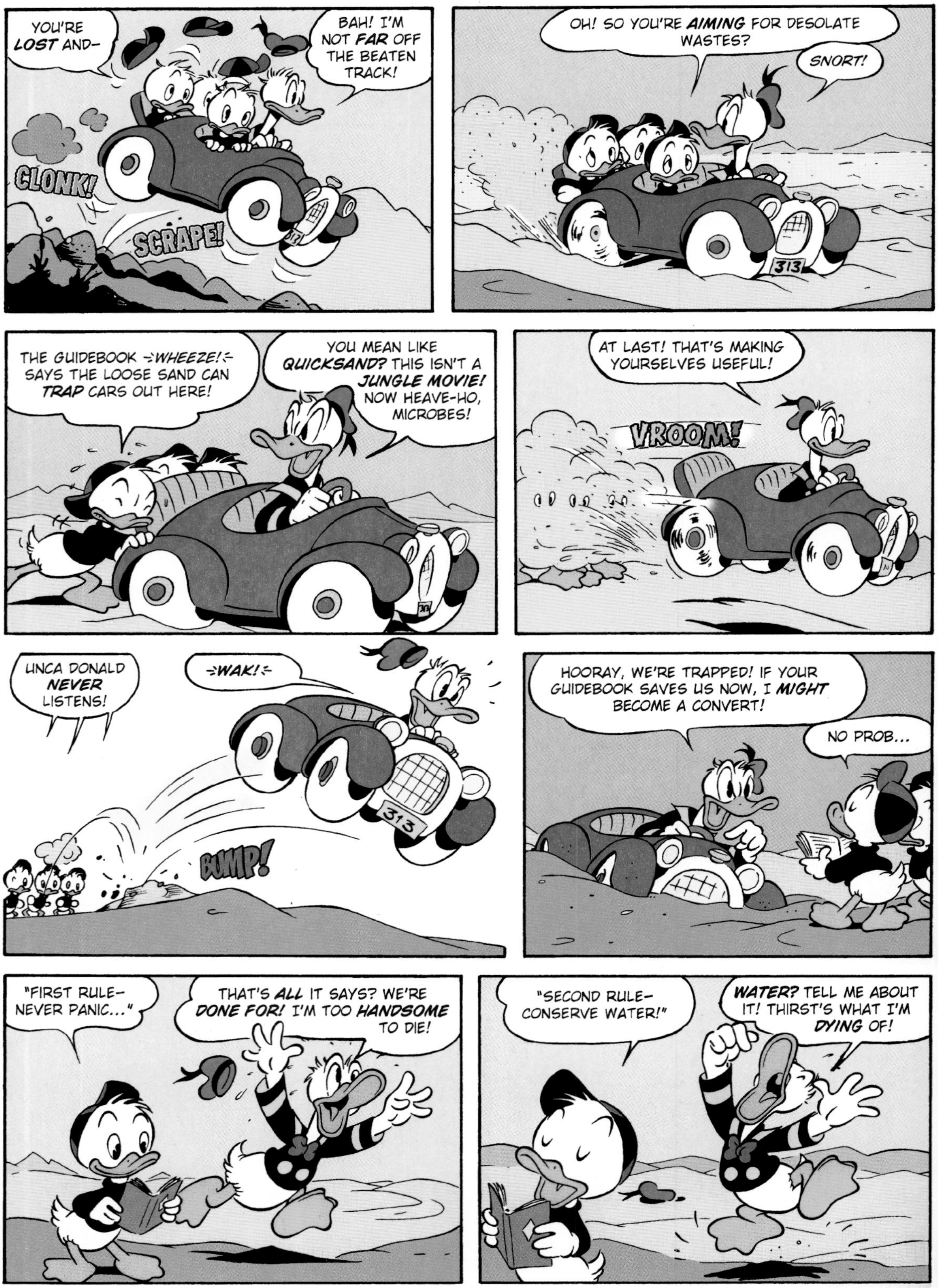
YOU'RE LOST AND–
BAH! I'M NOT FAR OFF THE BEATEN TRACK!
CLONK!
SCRAPE!
OH! SO YOU'RE AIMING FOR DESOLATE WASTES?
SNORT!
313
THE GUIDEBOOK –WHEEZE!– SAYS THE LOOSE SAND CAN TRAP CARS OUT HERE!
YOU MEAN LIKE QUICKSAND? THIS ISN'T A JUNGLE MOVIE! NOW HEAVE-HO, MICROBES!
AT LAST! THAT'S MAKING YOURSELVES USEFUL!
VROOM!
UNCA DONALD NEVER LISTENS!
–WAK!–
313
BUMP!
HOORAY, WE'RE TRAPPED! IF YOUR GUIDEBOOK SAVES US NOW, I MIGHT BECOME A CONVERT!
NO PROB...
"FIRST RULE– NEVER PANIC..."
THAT'S ALL IT SAYS? WE'RE DONE FOR! I'M TOO HANDSOME TO DIE!
"SECOND RULE– CONSERVE WATER!"
WATER? TELL ME ABOUT IT! THIRST'S WHAT I'M DYING OF!

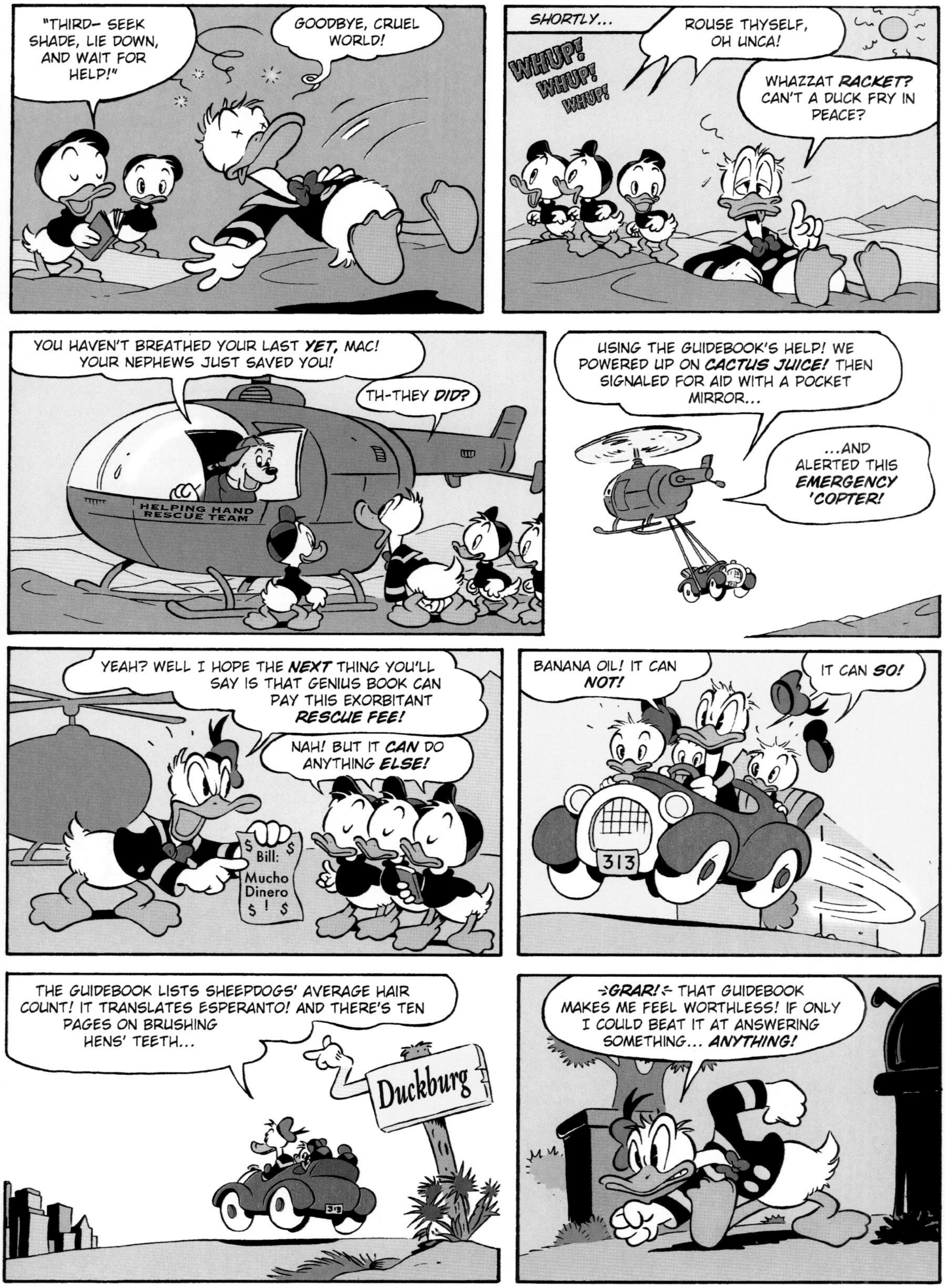
"THIRD– SEEK SHADE, LIE DOWN, AND WAIT FOR HELP!"
GOODBYE, CRUEL WORLD!
SHORTLY...
ROUSE THYSELF, OH UNCA!
WHUP! WHUP! WHUP!
WHAZZAT RACKET? CAN'T A DUCK FRY IN PEACE?
YOU HAVEN'T BREATHED YOUR LAST YET, MAC! YOUR NEPHEWS JUST SAVED YOU!
TH-THEY DID?
HELPING HAND RESCUE TEAM
USING THE GUIDEBOOK'S HELP! WE POWERED UP ON CACTUS JUICE! THEN SIGNALED FOR AID WITH A POCKET MIRROR...
...AND ALERTED THIS EMERGENCY 'COPTER!
YEAH? WELL I HOPE THE NEXT THING YOU'LL SAY IS THAT GENIUS BOOK CAN PAY THIS EXORBITANT RESCUE FEE!
NAH! BUT IT CAN DO ANYTHING ELSE!
$ Bill: $ Mucho Dinero $! $
BANANA OIL! IT CAN NOT!
IT CAN SO!
313
THE GUIDEBOOK LISTS SHEEPDOGS' AVERAGE HAIR COUNT! IT TRANSLATES ESPERANTO! AND THERE'S TEN PAGES ON BRUSHING HENS' TEETH...
Duckburg
GRAR! THAT GUIDEBOOK MAKES ME FEEL WORTHLESS! IF ONLY I COULD BEAT IT AT ANSWERING SOMETHING... ANYTHING!

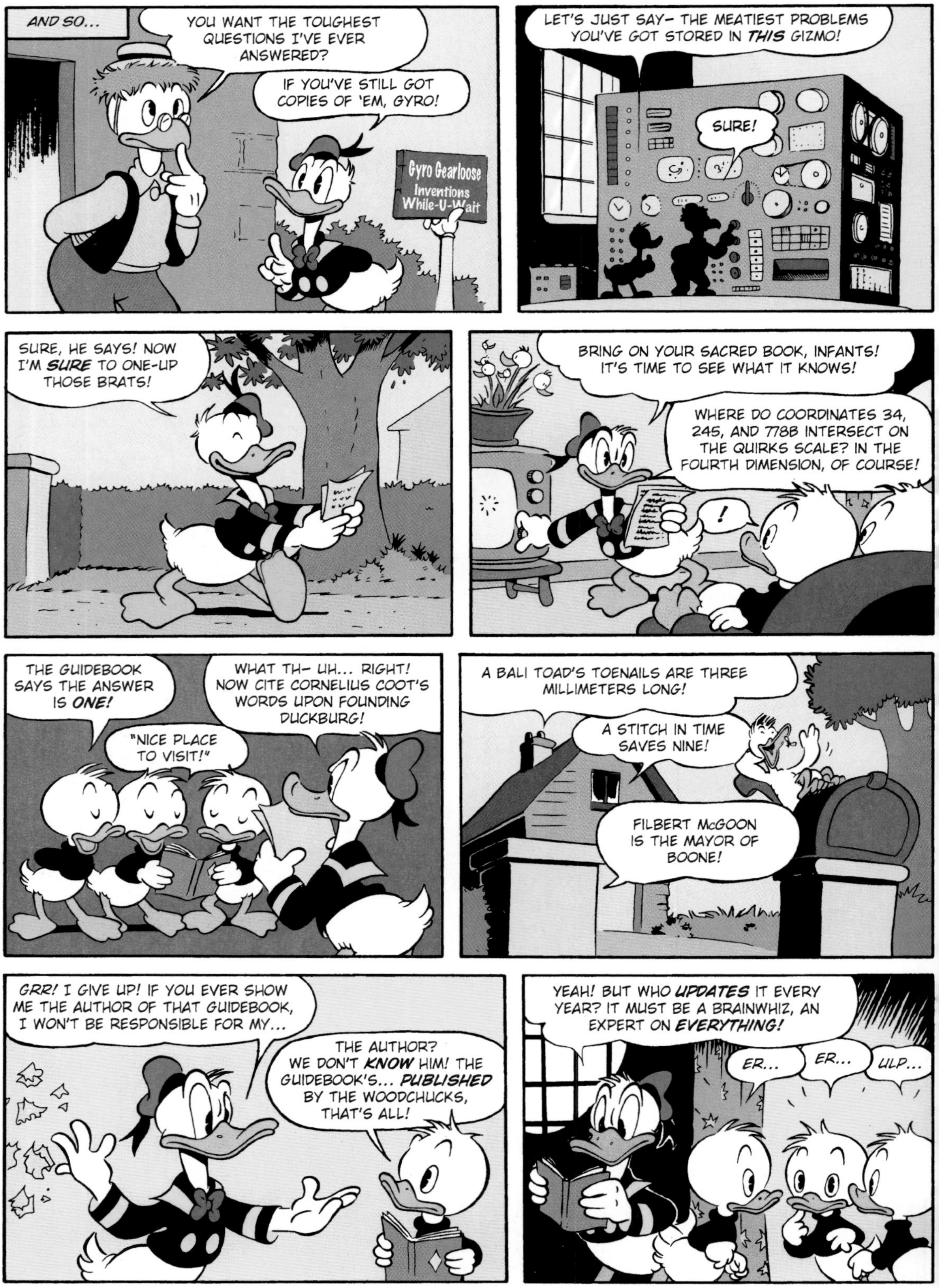
AND SO...
YOU WANT THE TOUGHEST QUESTIONS I'VE EVER ANSWERED?
IF YOU'VE STILL GOT COPIES OF 'EM, GYRO!
Gyro Gearloose Inventions While-U-Wait
LET'S JUST SAY– THE MEATIEST PROBLEMS YOU'VE GOT STORED IN THIS GIZMO!
SURE!
SURE, HE SAYS! NOW I'M SURE TO ONE-UP THOSE BRATS!
BRING ON YOUR SACRED BOOK, INFANTS! IT'S TIME TO SEE WHAT IT KNOWS!
WHERE DO COORDINATES 34, 245, AND 778B INTERSECT ON THE QUIRKS SCALE? IN THE FOURTH DIMENSION, OF COURSE!
!
THE GUIDEBOOK SAYS THE ANSWER IS ONE!
WHAT TH– UH... RIGHT! NOW CITE CORNELIUS COOT'S WORDS UPON FOUNDING DUCKBURG!
"NICE PLACE TO VISIT!"
A BALI TOAD'S TOENAILS ARE THREE MILLIMETERS LONG!
A STITCH IN TIME SAVES NINE!
FILBERT McGOON IS THE MAYOR OF BOONE!
GRR! I GIVE UP! IF YOU EVER SHOW ME THE AUTHOR OF THAT GUIDEBOOK, I WON'T BE RESPONSIBLE FOR MY...
THE AUTHOR? WE DON'T KNOW HIM! THE GUIDEBOOK'S... PUBLISHED BY THE WOODCHUCKS, THAT'S ALL!
YEAH! BUT WHO UPDATES IT EVERY YEAR? IT MUST BE A BRAINWHIZ, AN EXPERT ON EVERYTHING!
ER...
ER...
ULP...

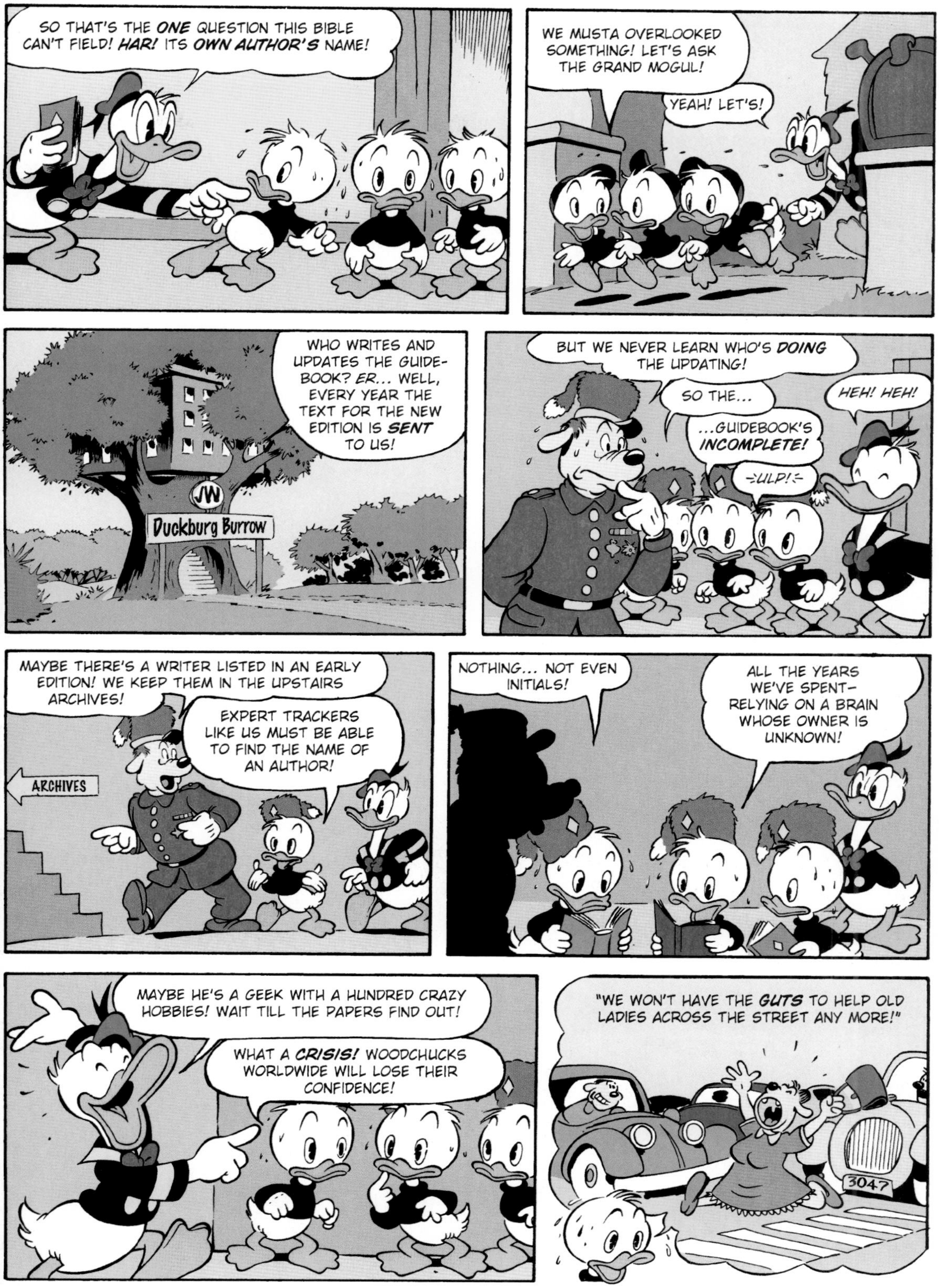
SO THAT'S THE ONE QUESTION THIS BIBLE CAN'T FIELD! HAR! ITS OWN AUTHOR'S NAME!
WE MUSTA OVERLOOKED SOMETHING! LET'S ASK THE GRAND MOGUL!
YEAH! LET'S!
Duckburg Burrow
JW
WHO WRITES AND UPDATES THE GUIDE-BOOK? ER... WELL, EVERY YEAR THE TEXT FOR THE NEW EDITION IS SENT TO US!
BUT WE NEVER LEARN WHO'S DOING THE UPDATING!
SO THE...
...GUIDEBOOK'S INCOMPLETE!
ULP!
HEH! HEH!
MAYBE THERE'S A WRITER LISTED IN AN EARLY EDITION! WE KEEP THEM IN THE UPSTAIRS ARCHIVES!
ARCHIVES
EXPERT TRACKERS LIKE US MUST BE ABLE TO FIND THE NAME OF AN AUTHOR!
NOTHING... NOT EVEN INITIALS!
ALL THE YEARS WE'VE SPENT— RELYING ON A BRAIN WHOSE OWNER IS UNKNOWN!
MAYBE HE'S A GEEK WITH A HUNDRED CRAZY HOBBIES! WAIT TILL THE PAPERS FIND OUT!
WHAT A CRISIS! WOODCHUCKS WORLDWIDE WILL LOSE THEIR CONFIDENCE!
"WE WON'T HAVE THE GUTS TO HELP OLD LADIES ACROSS THE STREET ANY MORE!"
3047

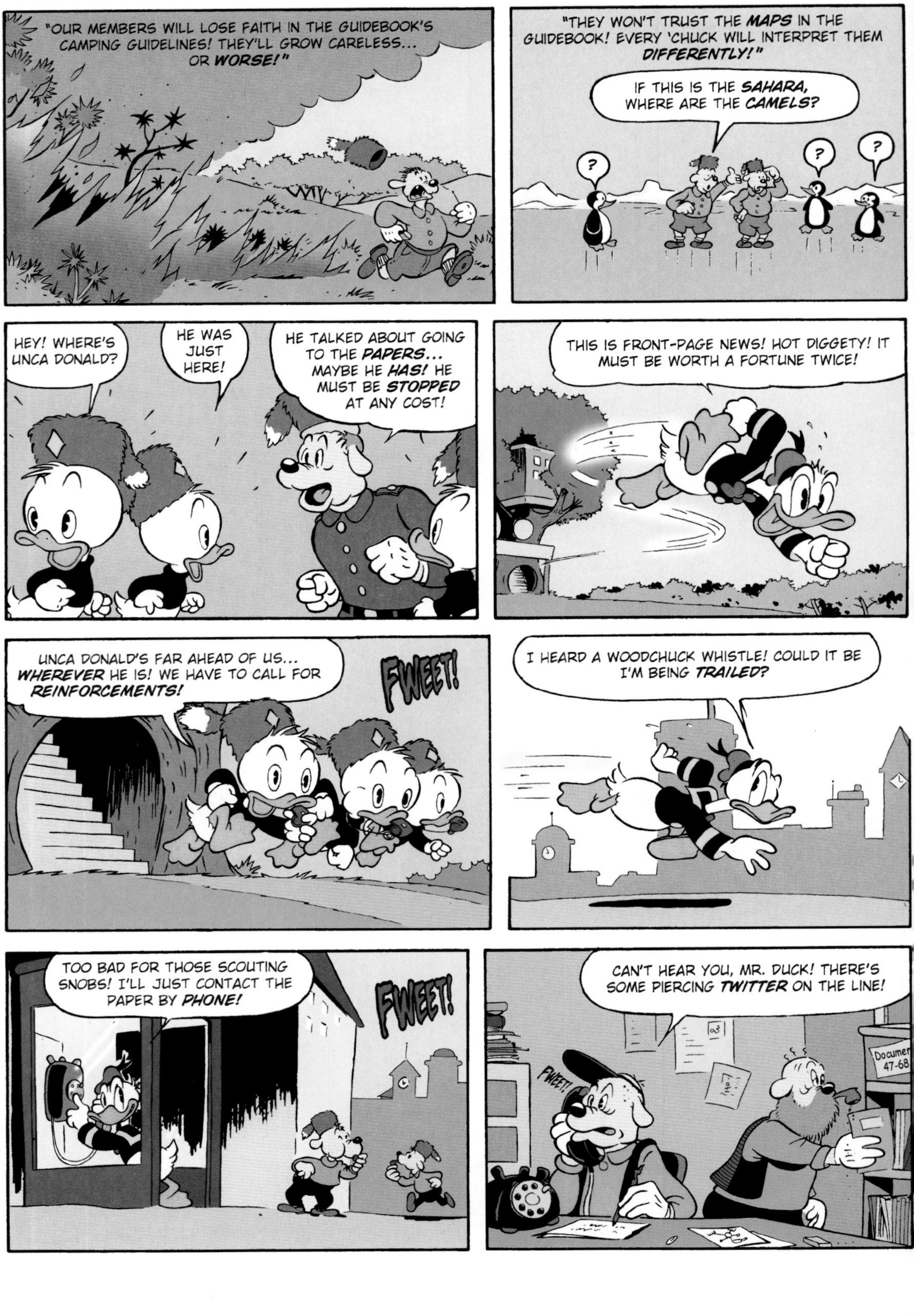
"OUR MEMBERS WILL LOSE FAITH IN THE GUIDEBOOK'S CAMPING GUIDELINES! THEY'LL GROW CARELESS... OR WORSE!"
"THEY WON'T TRUST THE MAPS IN THE GUIDEBOOK! EVERY 'CHUCK WILL INTERPRET THEM DIFFERENTLY!"
IF THIS IS THE SAHARA, WHERE ARE THE CAMELS?
?
?
?
HEY! WHERE'S UNCA DONALD?
HE WAS JUST HERE!
HE TALKED ABOUT GOING TO THE PAPERS... MAYBE HE HAS! HE MUST BE STOPPED AT ANY COST!
THIS IS FRONT-PAGE NEWS! HOT DIGGETY! IT MUST BE WORTH A FORTUNE TWICE!
UNCA DONALD'S FAR AHEAD OF US... WHEREVER HE IS! WE HAVE TO CALL FOR REINFORCEMENTS!
FWEET!
I HEARD A WOODCHUCK WHISTLE! COULD IT BE I'M BEING TRAILED?
TOO BAD FOR THOSE SCOUTING SNOBS! I'LL JUST CONTACT THE PAPER BY PHONE!
FWEET!
CAN'T HEAR YOU, MR. DUCK! THERE'S SOME PIERCING TWITTER ON THE LINE!
FWEET!
Documen 47-68

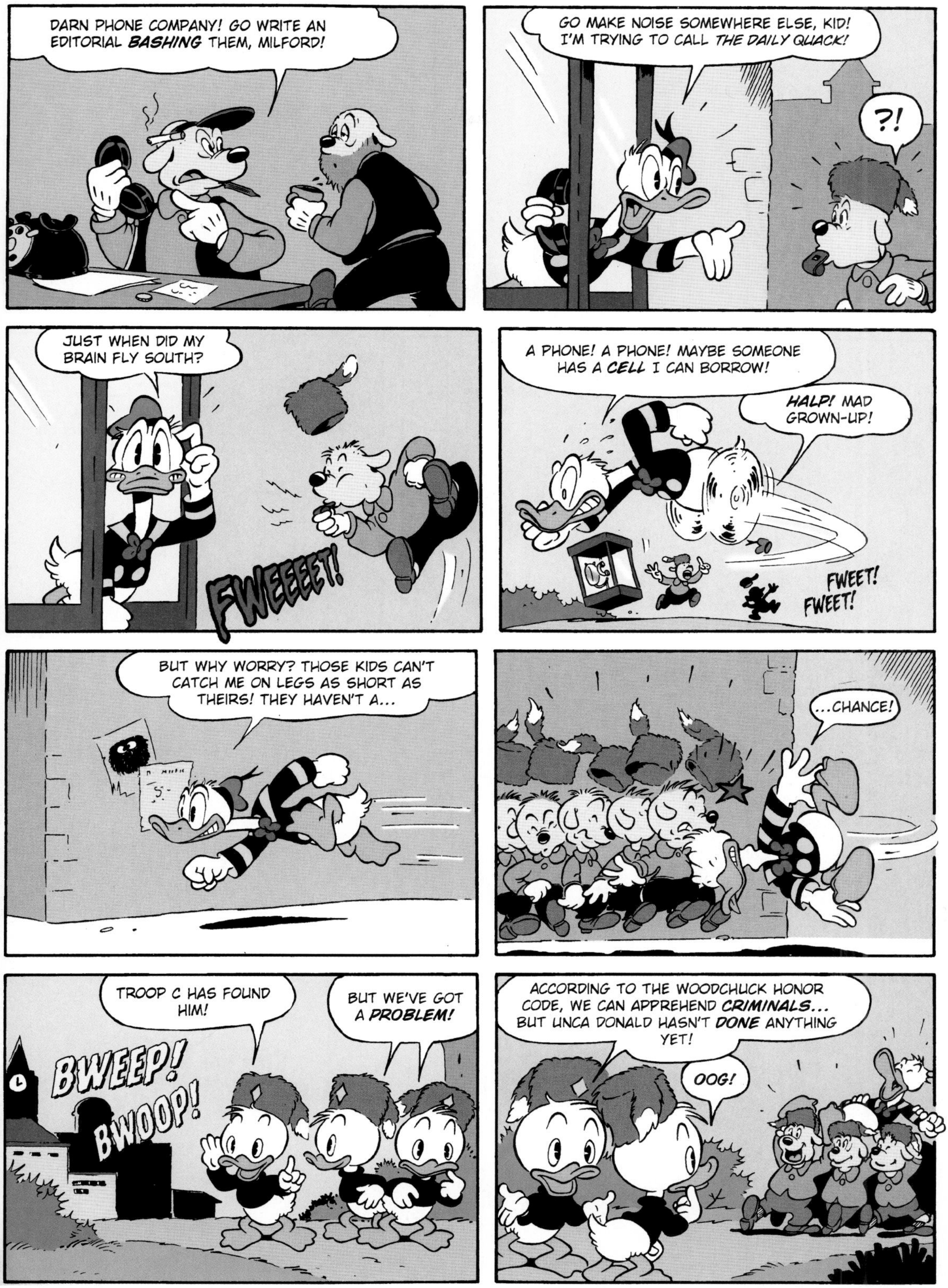
DARN PHONE COMPANY! GO WRITE AN EDITORIAL BASHING THEM, MILFORD!
GO MAKE NOISE SOMEWHERE ELSE, KID! I'M TRYING TO CALL THE DAILY QUACK!
?!
JUST WHEN DID MY BRAIN FLY SOUTH?
FWEEEEET!
A PHONE! A PHONE! MAYBE SOMEONE HAS A CELL I CAN BORROW!
HALP! MAD GROWN-UP!
FWEET! FWEET!
BUT WHY WORRY? THOSE KIDS CAN'T CATCH ME ON LEGS AS SHORT AS THEIRS! THEY HAVEN'T A...
...CHANCE!
TROOP C HAS FOUND HIM!
BUT WE'VE GOT A PROBLEM!
BWEEP! BWOOP!
ACCORDING TO THE WOODCHUCK HONOR CODE, WE CAN APPREHEND CRIMINALS... BUT UNCA DONALD HASN'T DONE ANYTHING YET!
OOG!

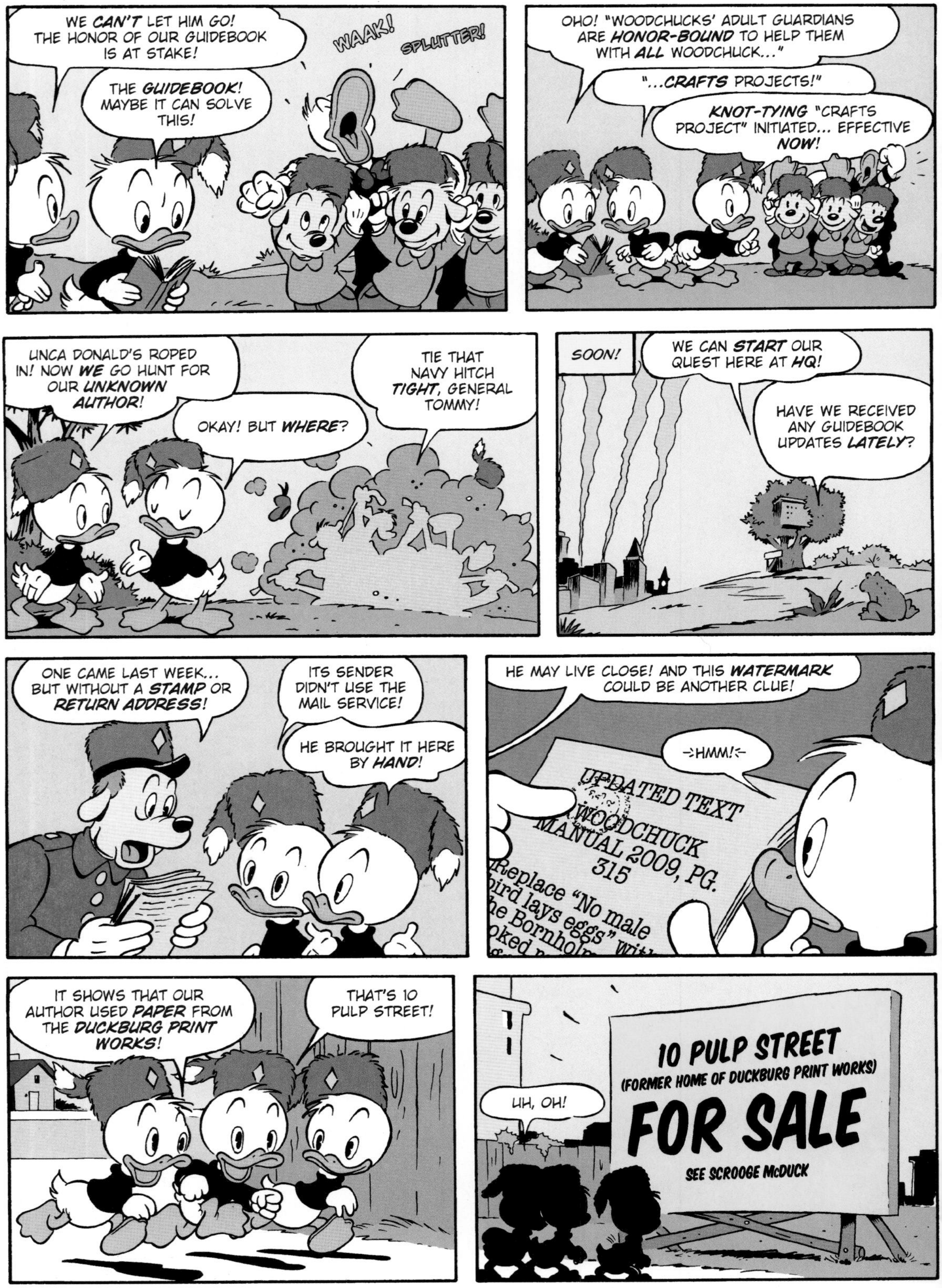
WE CAN'T LET HIM GO! THE HONOR OF OUR GUIDEBOOK IS AT STAKE!
THE GUIDEBOOK! MAYBE IT CAN SOLVE THIS!
WAAK!
SPLUTTER!
OHO! "WOODCHUCKS' ADULT GUARDIANS ARE HONOR-BOUND TO HELP THEM WITH ALL WOODCHUCK..."
"...CRAFTS PROJECTS!"
KNOT-TYING "CRAFTS PROJECT" INITIATED... EFFECTIVE NOW!
UNCA DONALD'S ROPED IN! NOW WE GO HUNT FOR OUR UNKNOWN AUTHOR!
OKAY! BUT WHERE?
TIE THAT NAVY HITCH TIGHT, GENERAL TOMMY!
SOON!
WE CAN START OUR QUEST HERE AT HQ!
HAVE WE RECEIVED ANY GUIDEBOOK UPDATES LATELY?
ONE CAME LAST WEEK... BUT WITHOUT A STAMP OR RETURN ADDRESS!
ITS SENDER DIDN'T USE THE MAIL SERVICE!
HE BROUGHT IT HERE BY HAND!
HE MAY LIVE CLOSE! AND THIS WATERMARK COULD BE ANOTHER CLUE!
HMM!
UPDATED TEXT
WOODCHUCK MANUAL 2009, PG. 315
Replace "No male bird lays eggs" with the Bornholm
IT SHOWS THAT OUR AUTHOR USED PAPER FROM THE DUCKBURG PRINT WORKS!
THAT'S 10 PULP STREET!
UH, OH!
10 PULP STREET
(FORMER HOME OF DUCKBURG PRINT WORKS)
FOR SALE
SEE SCROOGE McDUCK

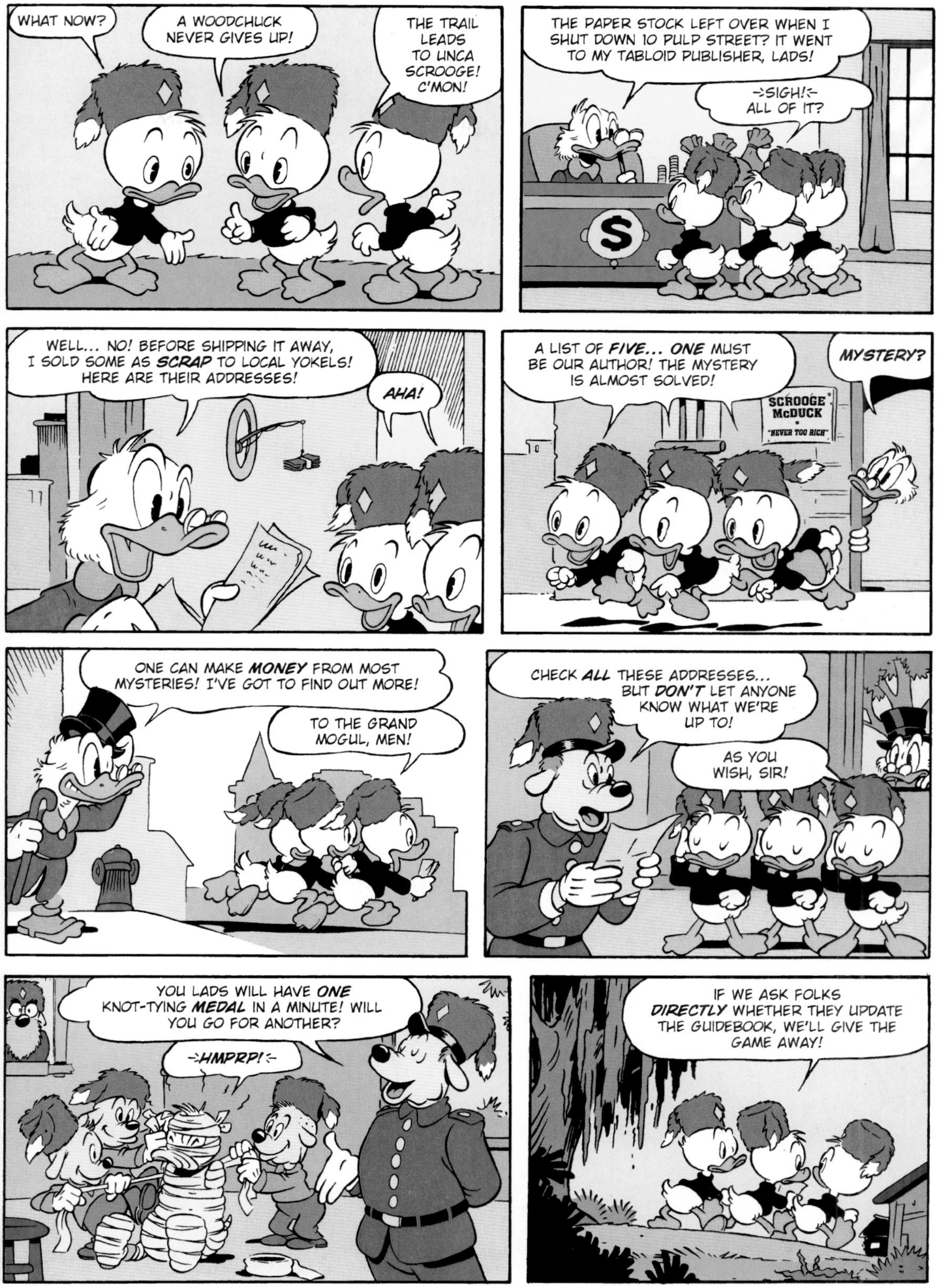
WHAT NOW?
A WOODCHUCK NEVER GIVES UP!
THE TRAIL LEADS TO UNCA SCROOGE! C'MON!
THE PAPER STOCK LEFT OVER WHEN I SHUT DOWN 10 PULP STREET? IT WENT TO MY TABLOID PUBLISHER, LADS!
-SIGH!- ALL OF IT?
WELL... NO! BEFORE SHIPPING IT AWAY, I SOLD SOME AS SCRAP TO LOCAL YOKELS! HERE ARE THEIR ADDRESSES!
AHA!
A LIST OF FIVE... ONE MUST BE OUR AUTHOR! THE MYSTERY IS ALMOST SOLVED!
MYSTERY?
SCROOGE McDUCK "NEVER TOO RICH"
ONE CAN MAKE MONEY FROM MOST MYSTERIES! I'VE GOT TO FIND OUT MORE!
TO THE GRAND MOGUL, MEN!
CHECK ALL THESE ADDRESSES... BUT DON'T LET ANYONE KNOW WHAT WE'RE UP TO!
AS YOU WISH, SIR!
YOU LADS WILL HAVE ONE KNOT-TYING MEDAL IN A MINUTE! WILL YOU GO FOR ANOTHER?
-HMPRP!-
IF WE ASK FOLKS DIRECTLY WHETHER THEY UPDATE THE GUIDEBOOK, WE'LL GIVE THE GAME AWAY!

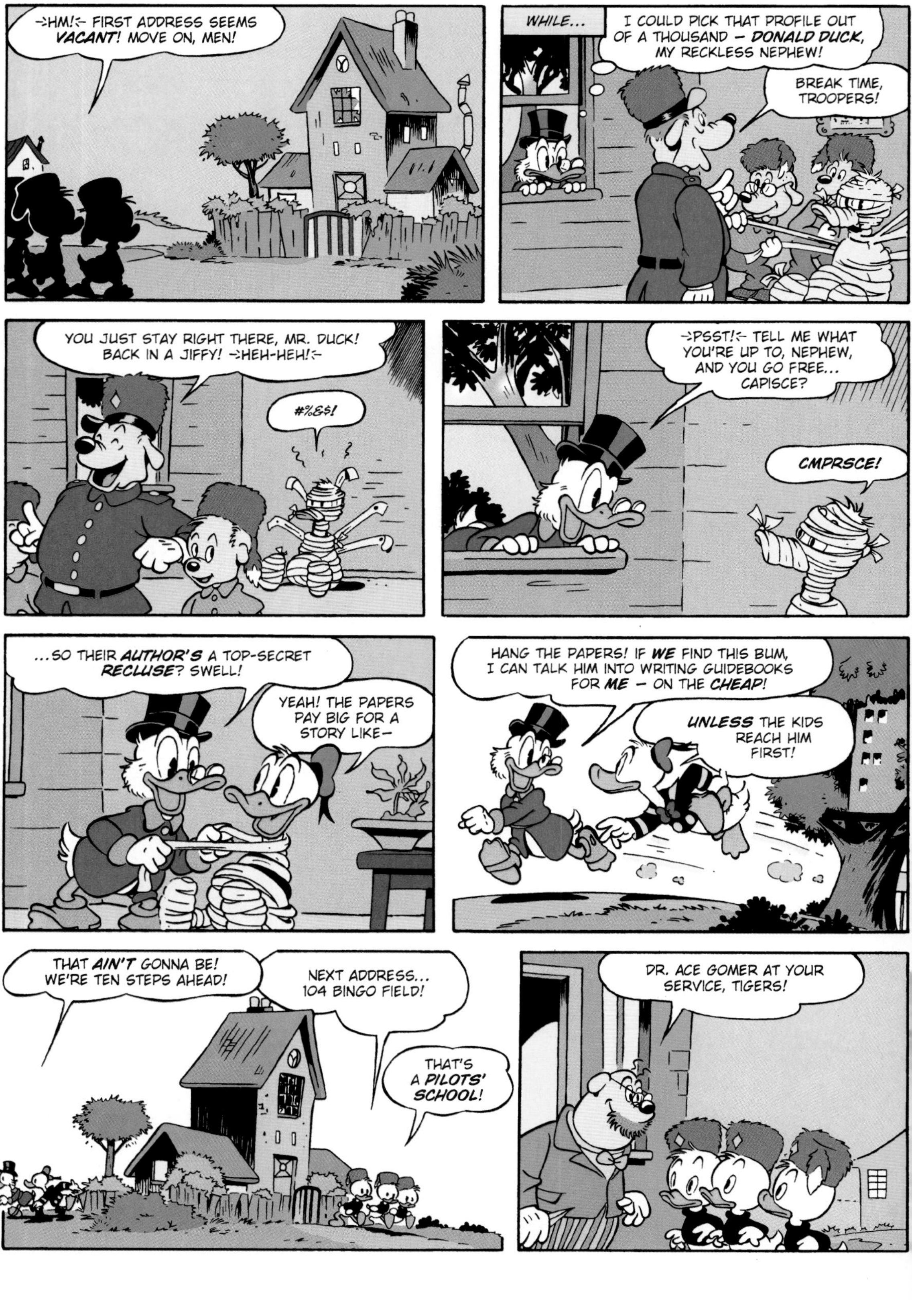

→HM!← FIRST ADDRESS SEEMS VACANT! MOVE ON, MEN!
WHILE...
I COULD PICK THAT PROFILE OUT OF A THOUSAND — DONALD DUCK, MY RECKLESS NEPHEW!
BREAK TIME, TROOPERS!
YOU JUST STAY RIGHT THERE, MR. DUCK! BACK IN A JIFFY! →HEH-HEH!←
#%&$!
→PSST!← TELL ME WHAT YOU'RE UP TO, NEPHEW, AND YOU GO FREE... CAPISCE?
CMPRSCE!
...SO THEIR AUTHOR'S A TOP-SECRET RECLUSE? SWELL!
YEAH! THE PAPERS PAY BIG FOR A STORY LIKE—
HANG THE PAPERS! IF WE FIND THIS BUM, I CAN TALK HIM INTO WRITING GUIDEBOOKS FOR ME — ON THE CHEAP!
UNLESS THE KIDS REACH HIM FIRST!
THAT AIN'T GONNA BE! WE'RE TEN STEPS AHEAD!
NEXT ADDRESS... 104 BINGO FIELD!
THAT'S A PILOTS' SCHOOL!
DR. ACE GOMER AT YOUR SERVICE, TIGERS!

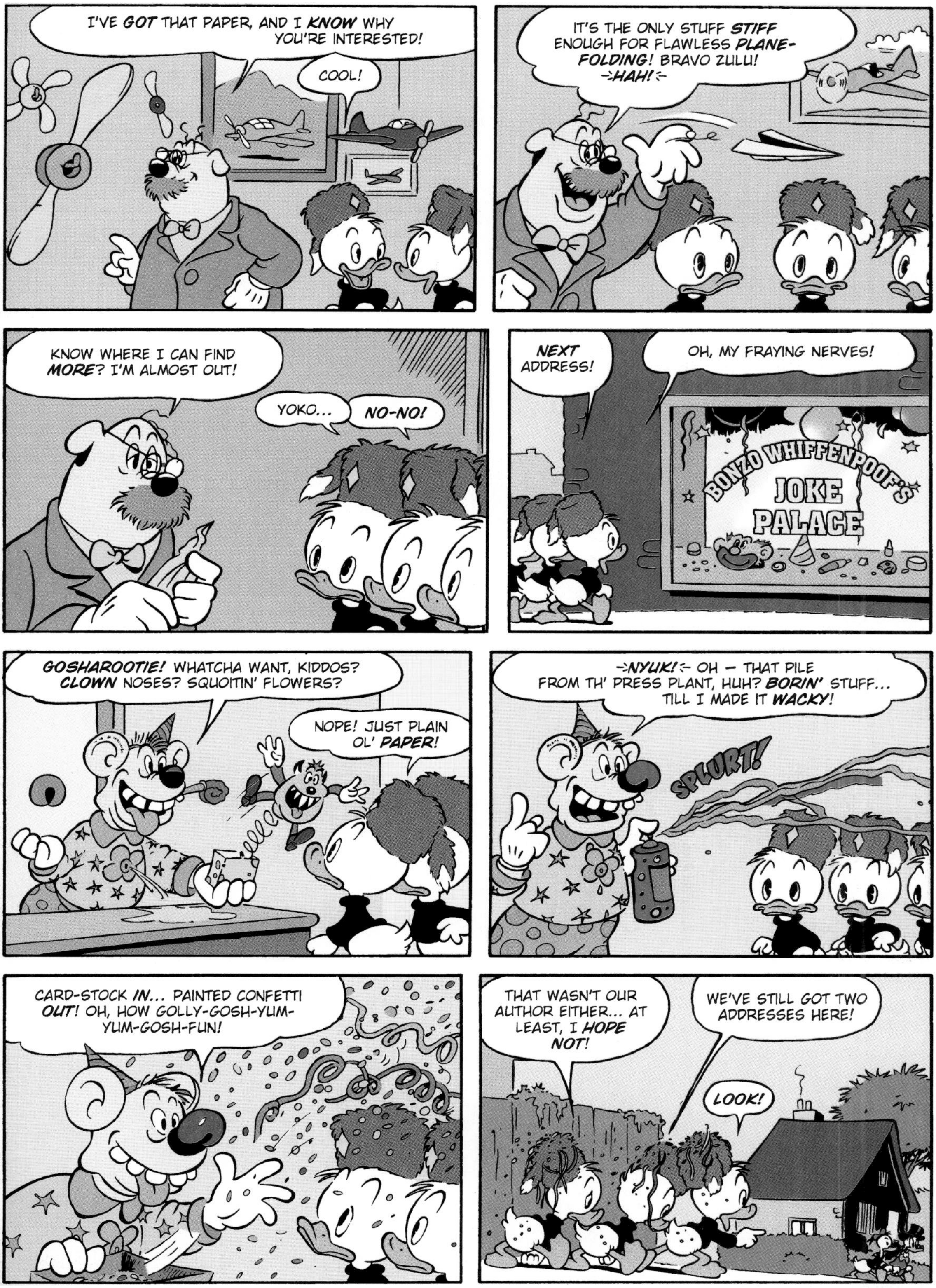

I'VE GOT THAT PAPER, AND I KNOW WHY YOU'RE INTERESTED!
COOL!
IT'S THE ONLY STUFF STIFF ENOUGH FOR FLAWLESS PLANE-FOLDING! BRAVO ZULU! HAH!
KNOW WHERE I CAN FIND MORE? I'M ALMOST OUT!
YOKO...
NO-NO!
NEXT ADDRESS!
OH, MY FRAYING NERVES!
BONZO WHIFFENPOOF'S JOKE PALACE
GOSHAROOTIE! WHATCHA WANT, KIDDOS? CLOWN NOSES? SQUOITIN' FLOWERS?
NOPE! JUST PLAIN OL' PAPER!
NYUK! OH — THAT PILE FROM TH' PRESS PLANT, HUH? BORIN' STUFF... TILL I MADE IT WACKY!
SPLURT!
CARD-STOCK IN... PAINTED CONFETTI OUT! OH, HOW GOLLY-GOSH-YUM-YUM-GOSH-FUN!
THAT WASN'T OUR AUTHOR EITHER... AT LEAST, I HOPE NOT!
WE'VE STILL GOT TWO ADDRESSES HERE!
LOOK!

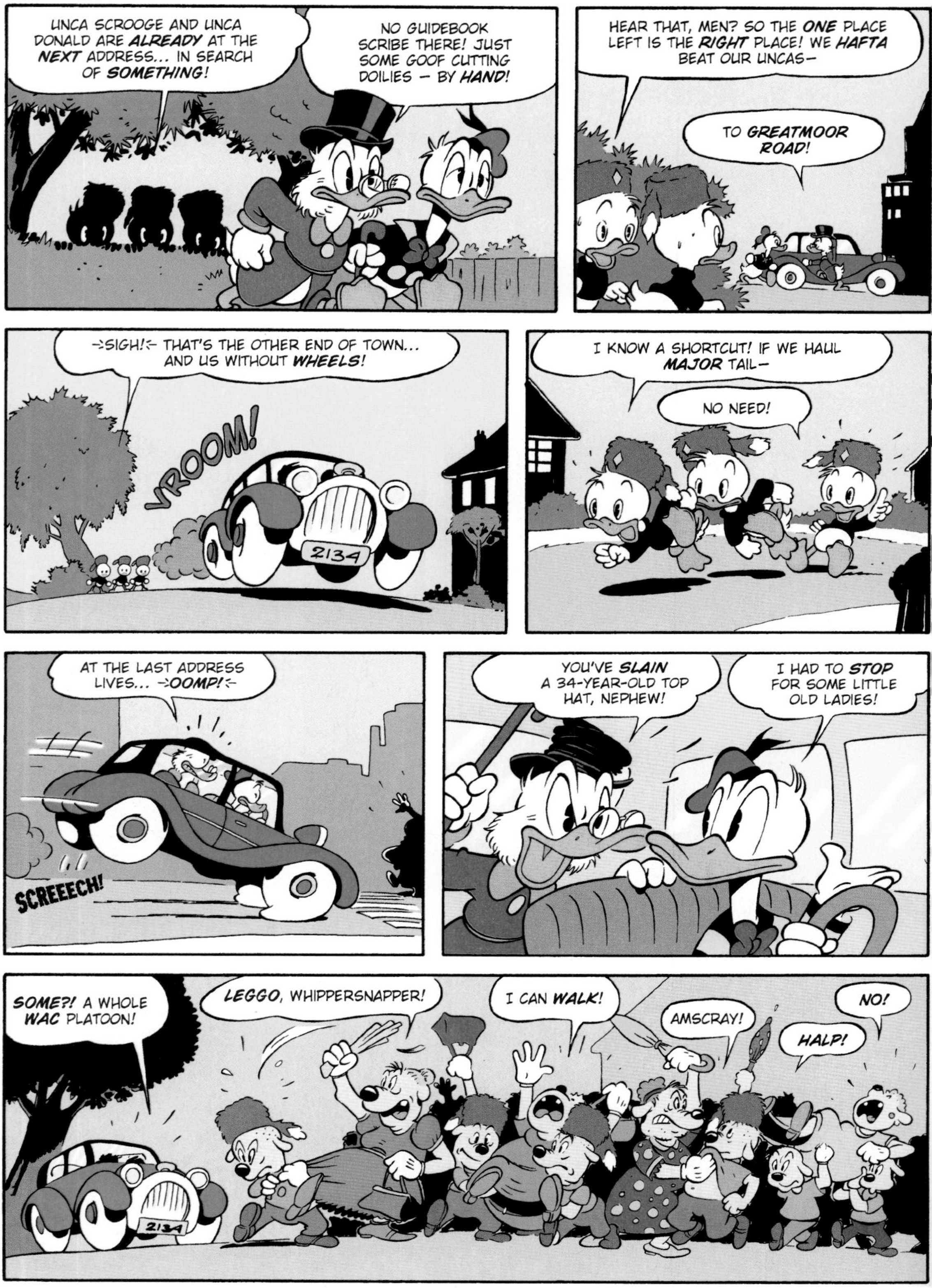
UNCA SCROOGE AND UNCA DONALD ARE ALREADY AT THE NEXT ADDRESS... IN SEARCH OF SOMETHING!
NO GUIDEBOOK SCRIBE THERE! JUST SOME GOOF CUTTING DOILIES — BY HAND!
HEAR THAT, MEN? SO THE ONE PLACE LEFT IS THE RIGHT PLACE! WE HAFTA BEAT OUR UNCAS—
TO GREATMOOR ROAD!
-SIGH!- THAT'S THE OTHER END OF TOWN... AND US WITHOUT WHEELS!
VROOM!
2134
I KNOW A SHORTCUT! IF WE HAUL MAJOR TAIL—
NO NEED!
AT THE LAST ADDRESS LIVES... -OOMP!-
SCREEECH!
YOU'VE SLAIN A 34-YEAR-OLD TOP HAT, NEPHEW!
I HAD TO STOP FOR SOME LITTLE OLD LADIES!
SOME?! A WHOLE WAC PLATOON!
LEGGO, WHIPPERSNAPPER!
I CAN WALK!
AMSCRAY!
NO!
HALP!
2134

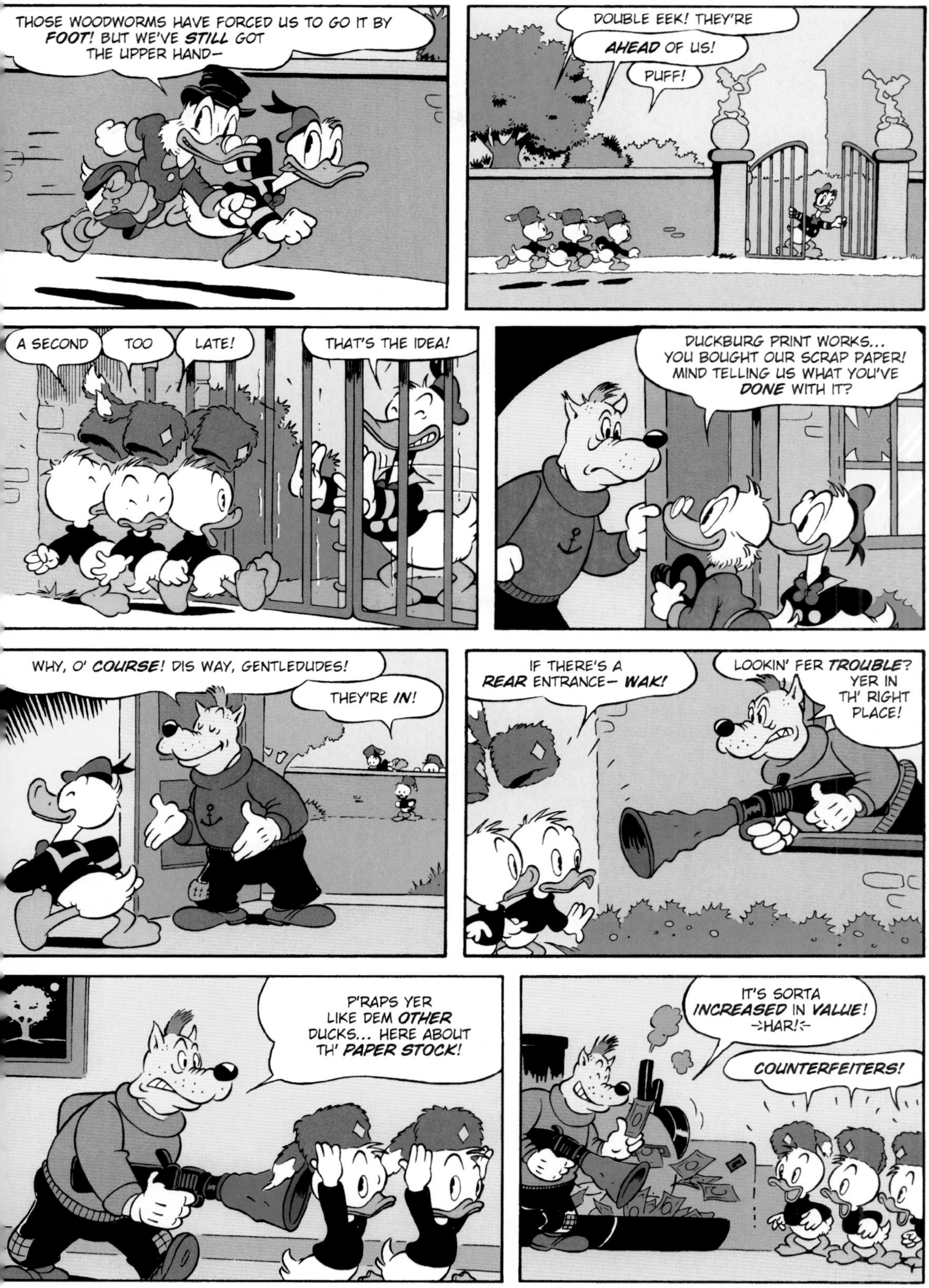

THOSE WOODWORMS HAVE FORCED US TO GO IT BY FOOT! BUT WE'VE STILL GOT THE UPPER HAND—
DOUBLE EEK! THEY'RE
AHEAD OF US!
PUFF!
A SECOND
TOO
LATE!
THAT'S THE IDEA!
DUCKBURG PRINT WORKS... YOU BOUGHT OUR SCRAP PAPER! MIND TELLING US WHAT YOU'VE DONE WITH IT?
WHY, O' COURSE! DIS WAY, GENTLEDUDES!
THEY'RE IN!
IF THERE'S A REAR ENTRANCE— WAK!
LOOKIN' FER TROUBLE? YER IN TH' RIGHT PLACE!
P'RAPS YER LIKE DEM OTHER DUCKS... HERE ABOUT TH' PAPER STOCK!
IT'S SORTA INCREASED IN VALUE! HAR!
COUNTERFEITERS!

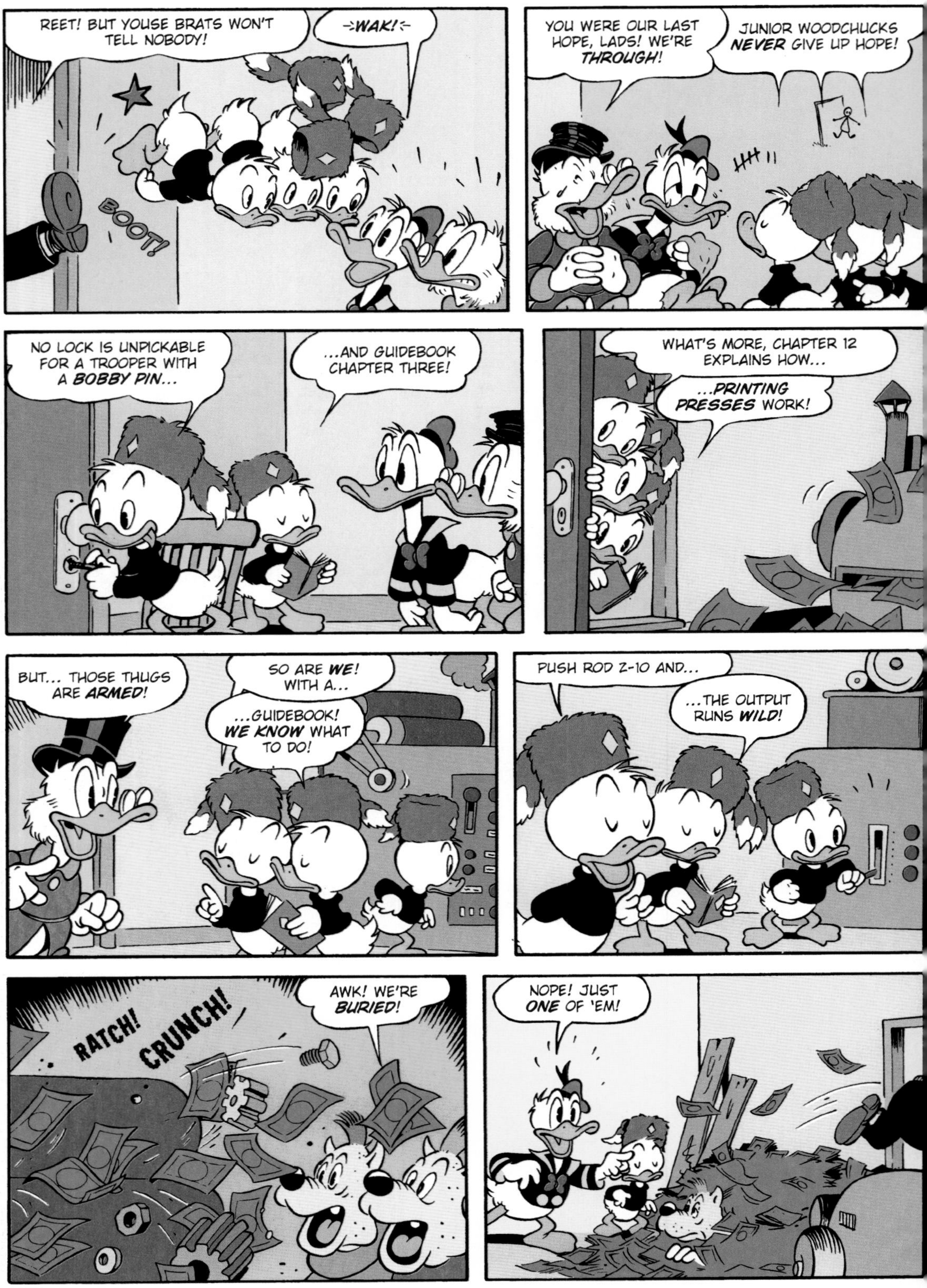
REET! BUT YOUSE BRATS WON'T TELL NOBODY!
-WAK!-
BOOT!
YOU WERE OUR LAST HOPE, LADS! WE'RE THROUGH!
JUNIOR WOODCHUCKS NEVER GIVE UP HOPE!
NO LOCK IS UNPICKABLE FOR A TROOPER WITH A BOBBY PIN...
...AND GUIDEBOOK CHAPTER THREE!
WHAT'S MORE, CHAPTER 12 EXPLAINS HOW...
...PRINTING PRESSES WORK!
BUT... THOSE THUGS ARE ARMED!
SO ARE WE! WITH A...
...GUIDEBOOK! WE KNOW WHAT TO DO!
PUSH ROD Z-10 AND...
...THE OUTPUT RUNS WILD!
RATCH!
CRUNCH!
AWK! WE'RE BURIED!
NOPE! JUST ONE OF 'EM!

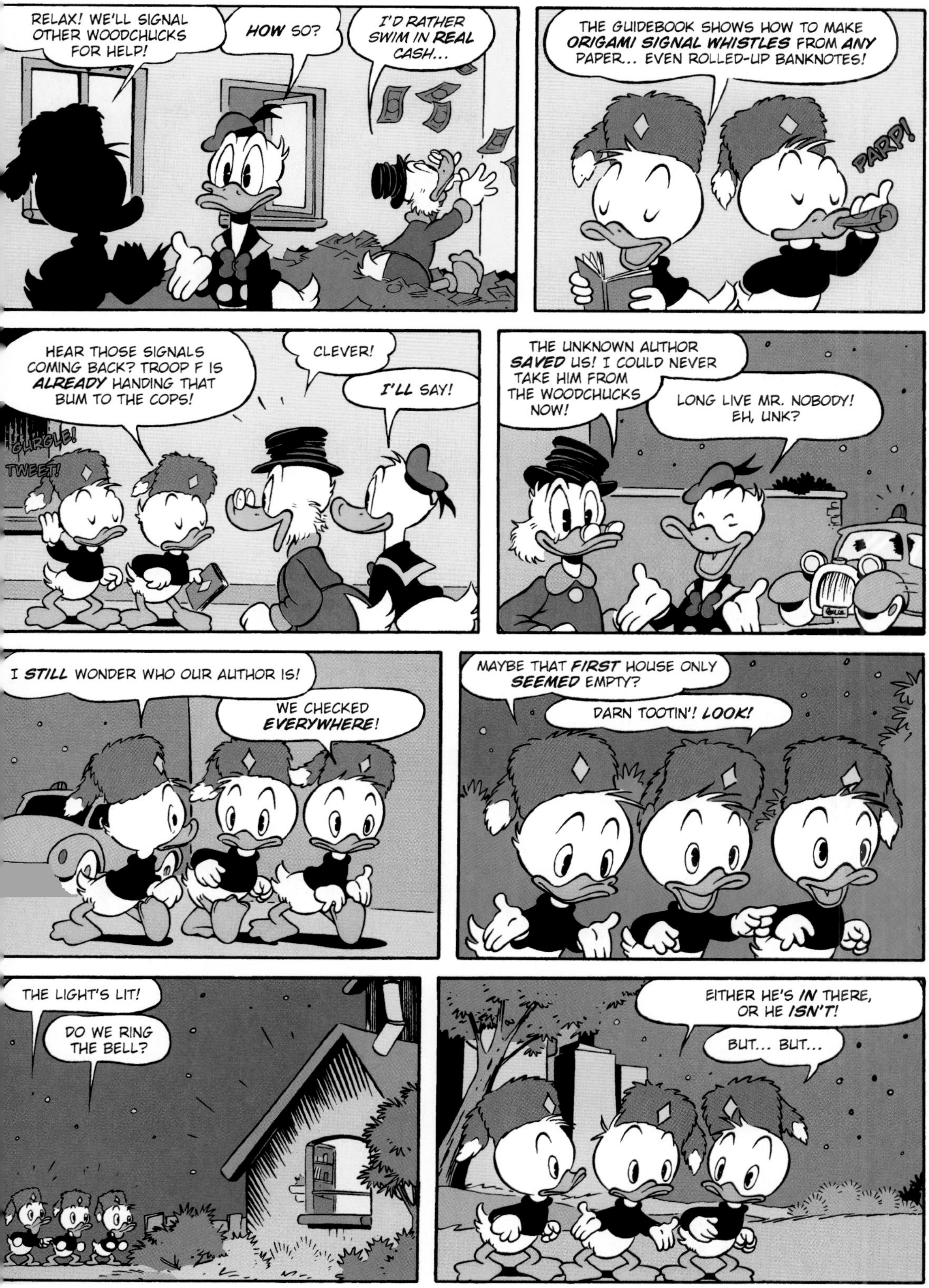
RELAX! WE'LL SIGNAL OTHER WOODCHUCKS FOR HELP!
HOW SO?
I'D RATHER SWIM IN REAL CASH...
THE GUIDEBOOK SHOWS HOW TO MAKE ORIGAMI SIGNAL WHISTLES FROM ANY PAPER... EVEN ROLLED-UP BANKNOTES!
PARP!
HEAR THOSE SIGNALS COMING BACK? TROOP F IS ALREADY HANDING THAT BUM TO THE COPS!
GURGLE!
TWEET!
CLEVER!
I'LL SAY!
THE UNKNOWN AUTHOR SAVED US! I COULD NEVER TAKE HIM FROM THE WOODCHUCKS NOW!
LONG LIVE MR. NOBODY! EH, UNK?
I STILL WONDER WHO OUR AUTHOR IS!
WE CHECKED EVERYWHERE!
MAYBE THAT FIRST HOUSE ONLY SEEMED EMPTY?
DARN TOOTIN'! LOOK!
THE LIGHT'S LIT!
DO WE RING THE BELL?
EITHER HE'S IN THERE, OR HE ISN'T!
BUT... BUT...

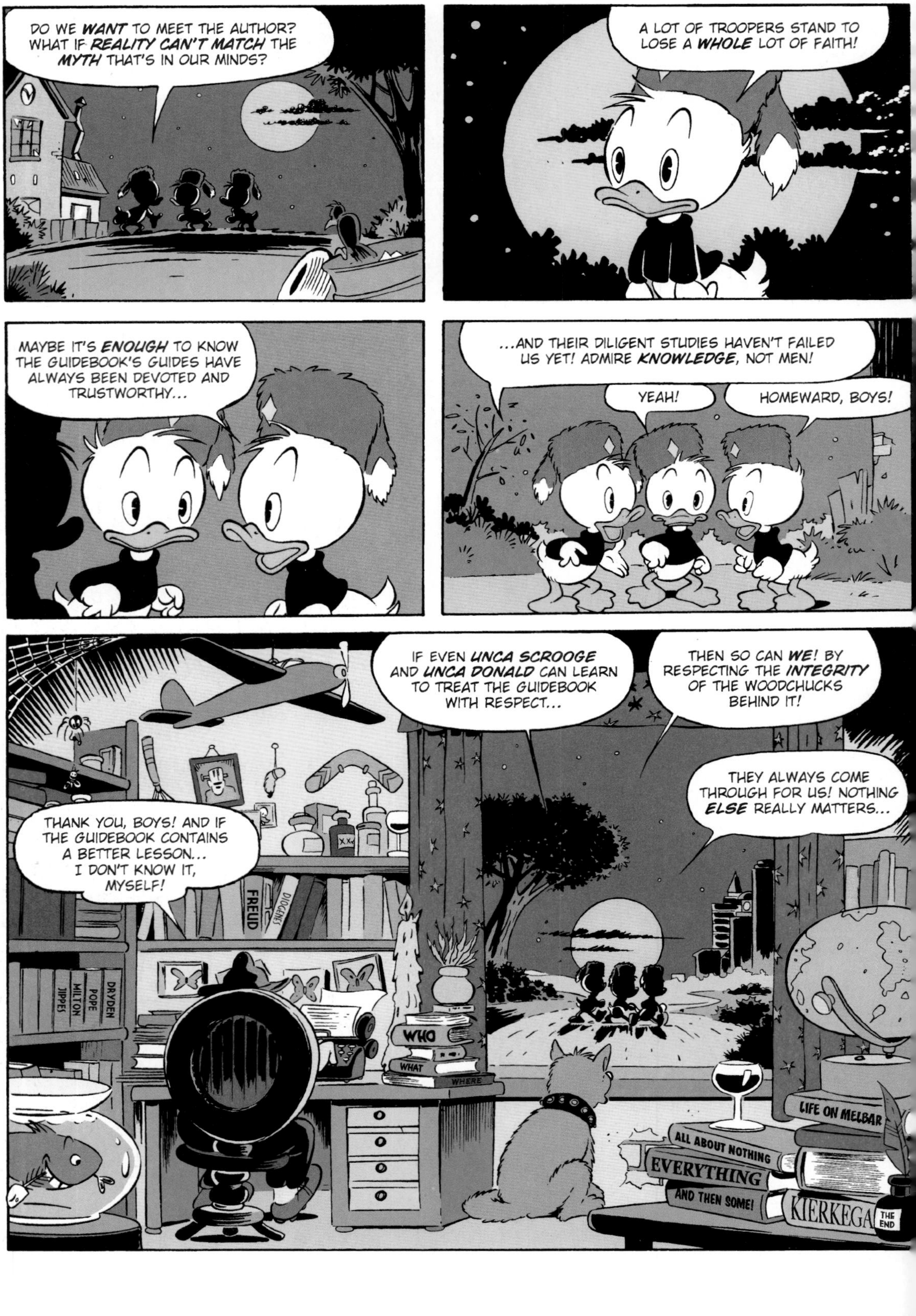
DO WE WANT TO MEET THE AUTHOR? WHAT IF REALITY CAN'T MATCH THE MYTH THAT'S IN OUR MINDS?
A LOT OF TROOPERS STAND TO LOSE A WHOLE LOT OF FAITH!
MAYBE IT'S ENOUGH TO KNOW THE GUIDEBOOK'S GUIDES HAVE ALWAYS BEEN DEVOTED AND TRUSTWORTHY...
...AND THEIR DILIGENT STUDIES HAVEN'T FAILED US YET! ADMIRE KNOWLEDGE, NOT MEN!
YEAH!
HOMEWARD, BOYS!
IF EVEN UNCA SCROOGE AND UNCA DONALD CAN LEARN TO TREAT THE GUIDEBOOK WITH RESPECT...
THEN SO CAN WE! BY RESPECTING THE INTEGRITY OF THE WOODCHUCKS BEHIND IT!
THEY ALWAYS COME THROUGH FOR US! NOTHING ELSE REALLY MATTERS...
THANK YOU, BOYS! AND IF THE GUIDEBOOK CONTAINS A BETTER LESSON... I DON'T KNOW IT, MYSELF!
FREUD
DIOGENES
JIPPES
MILTON
POPE
DRYDEN
WHO
WHAT
WHERE
LIFE ON MELBAR
ALL ABOUT NOTHING
EVERYTHING
AND THEN SOME!
KIERKEGA
THE END

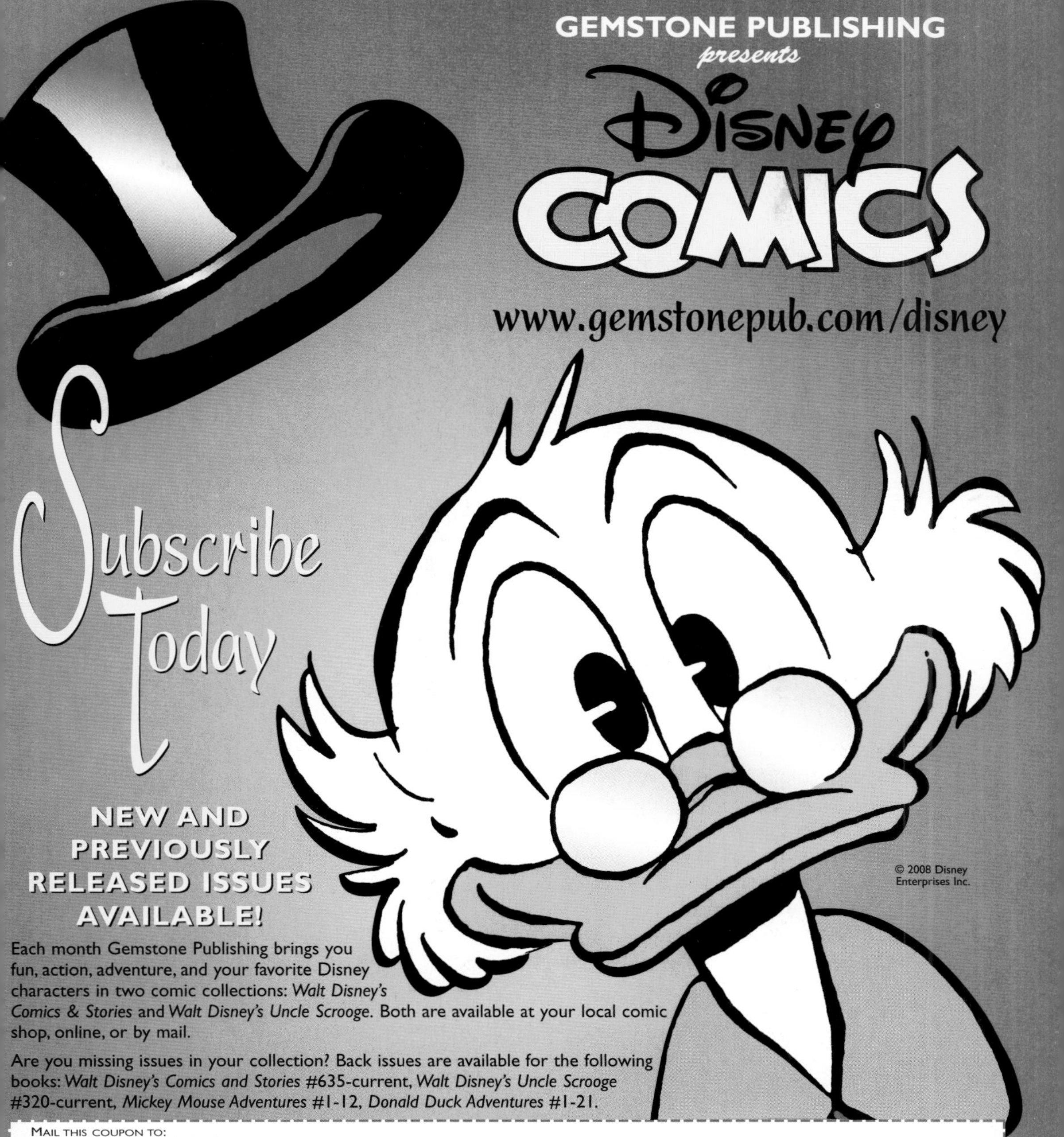

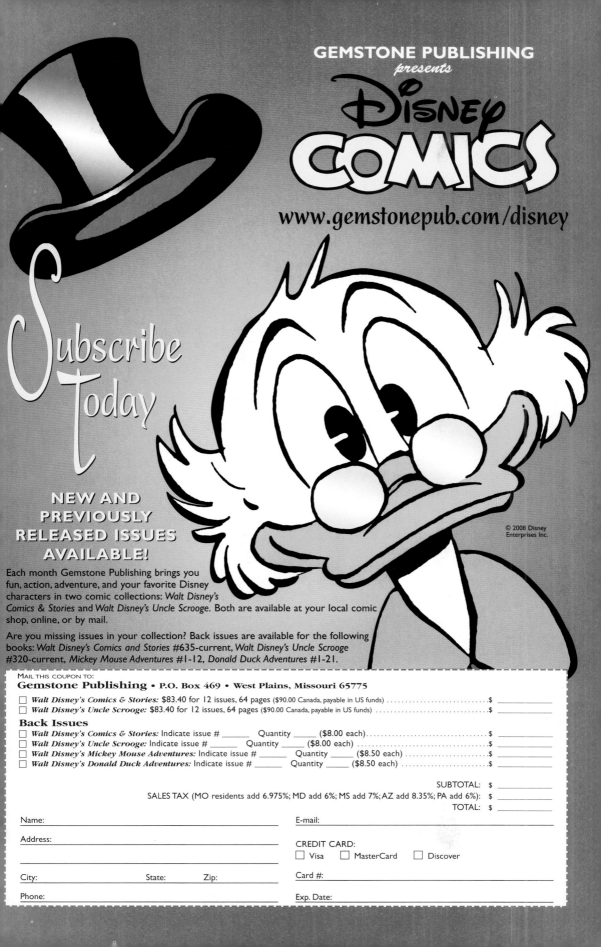

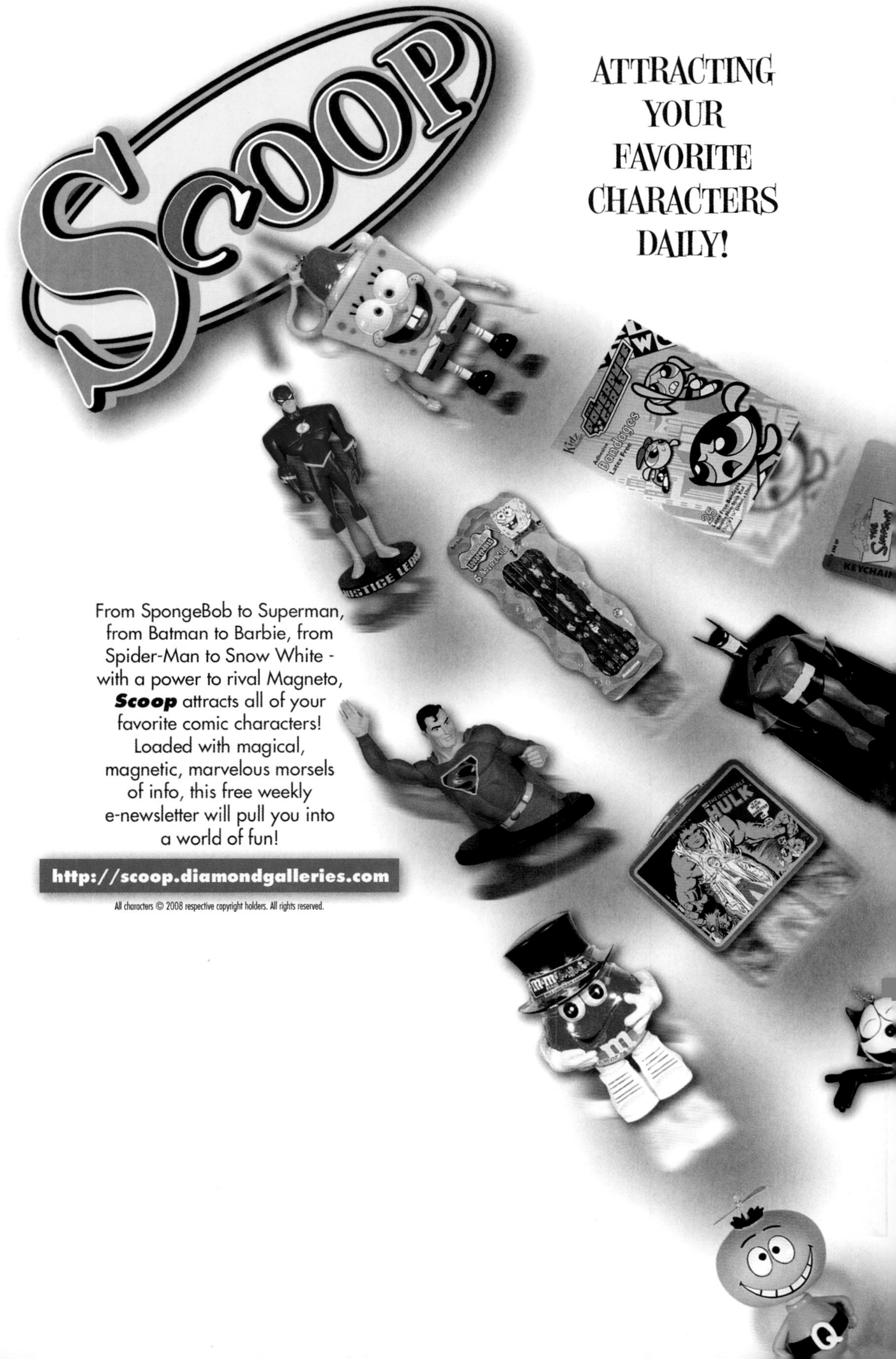

SCOOP
ATTRACTING YOUR FAVORITE CHARACTERS DAILY!
From SpongeBob to Superman, from Batman to Barbie, from Spider-Man to Snow White - with a power to rival Magneto, **Scoop** attracts all of your favorite comic characters! Loaded with magical, magnetic, marvelous morsels of info, this free weekly e-newsletter will pull you into a world of fun!
http://scoop.diamondgalleries.com
All characters © 2008 respective copyright holders. All rights reserved.

Walt Disney's Uncle $crooge in Senior Woodchuck

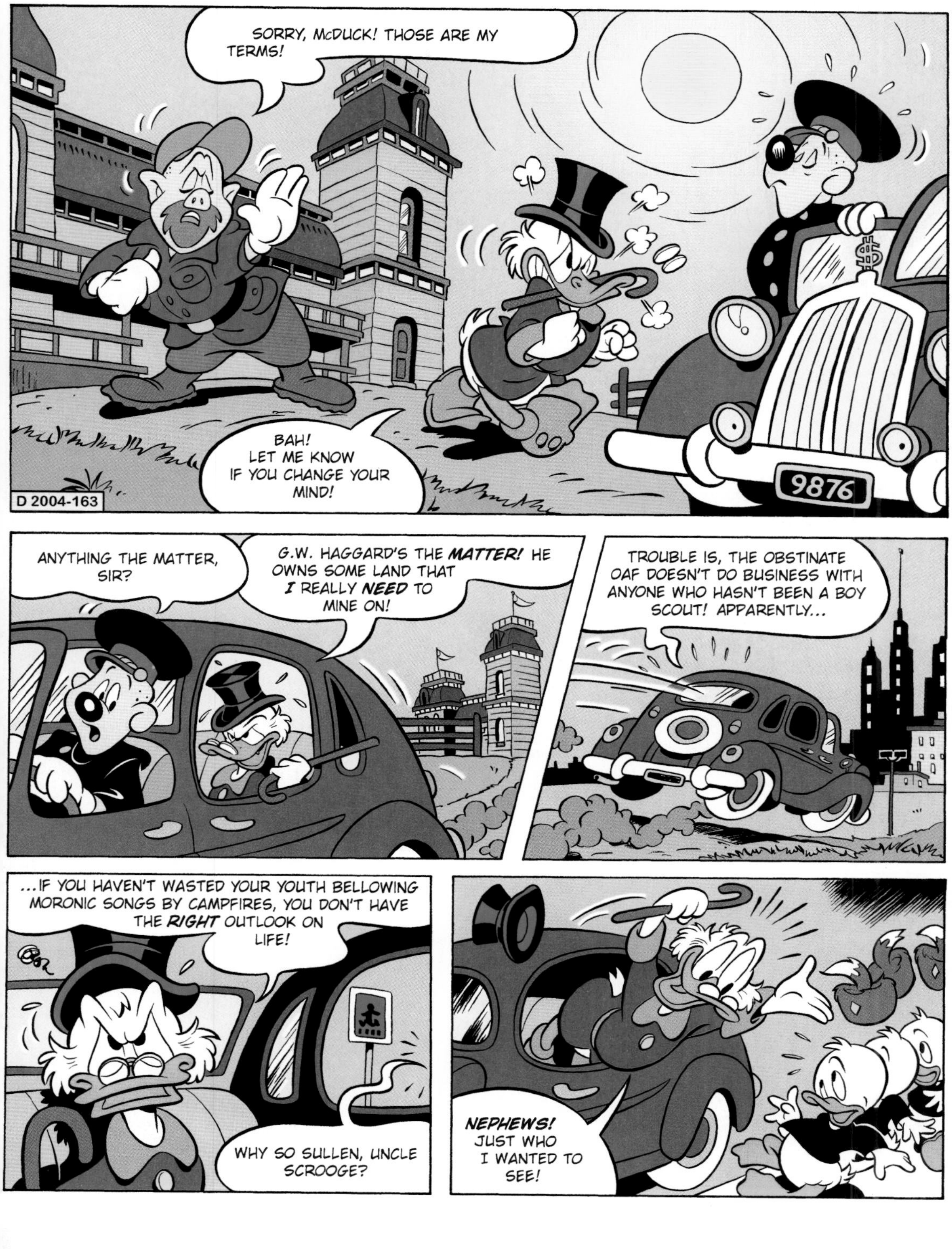

SORRY, McDUCK! THOSE ARE MY TERMS!
BAH! LET ME KNOW IF YOU CHANGE YOUR MIND!
D 2004-163
9876
ANYTHING THE MATTER, SIR?
G.W. HAGGARD'S THE **MATTER!** HE OWNS SOME LAND THAT ***I*** REALLY **NEED** TO MINE ON!
TROUBLE IS, THE OBSTINATE OAF DOESN'T DO BUSINESS WITH ANYONE WHO HASN'T BEEN A BOY SCOUT! APPARENTLY...
...IF YOU HAVEN'T WASTED YOUR YOUTH BELLOWING MORONIC SONGS BY CAMPFIRES, YOU DON'T HAVE THE **RIGHT** OUTLOOK ON LIFE!
WHY SO SULLEN, UNCLE SCROOGE?
NEPHEWS! JUST WHO I WANTED TO SEE!

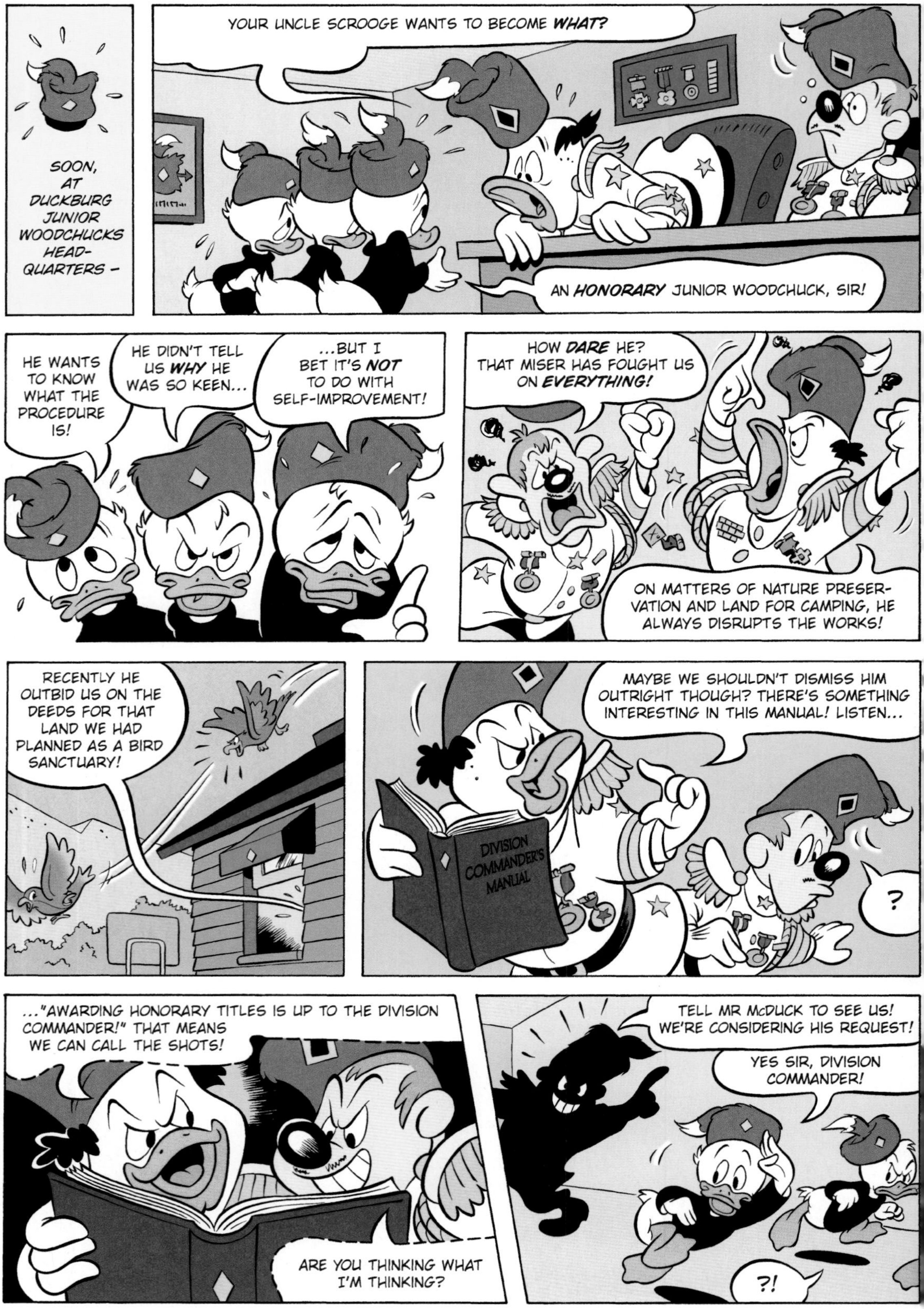
SOON, AT DUCKBURG JUNIOR WOODCHUCKS HEAD-QUARTERS –
YOUR UNCLE SCROOGE WANTS TO BECOME WHAT?
AN HONORARY JUNIOR WOODCHUCK, SIR!
HE WANTS TO KNOW WHAT THE PROCEDURE IS!
HE DIDN'T TELL US WHY HE WAS SO KEEN...
...BUT I BET IT'S NOT TO DO WITH SELF-IMPROVEMENT!
HOW DARE HE? THAT MISER HAS FOUGHT US ON EVERYTHING!
ON MATTERS OF NATURE PRESER-VATION AND LAND FOR CAMPING, HE ALWAYS DISRUPTS THE WORKS!
RECENTLY HE OUTBID US ON THE DEEDS FOR THAT LAND WE HAD PLANNED AS A BIRD SANCTUARY!
MAYBE WE SHOULDN'T DISMISS HIM OUTRIGHT THOUGH? THERE'S SOMETHING INTERESTING IN THIS MANUAL! LISTEN...
DIVISION COMMANDER'S MANUAL
?
..."AWARDING HONORARY TITLES IS UP TO THE DIVISION COMMANDER!" THAT MEANS WE CAN CALL THE SHOTS!
ARE YOU THINKING WHAT I'M THINKING?
TELL MR McDUCK TO SEE US! WE'RE CONSIDERING HIS REQUEST!
YES SIR, DIVISION COMMANDER!
?!

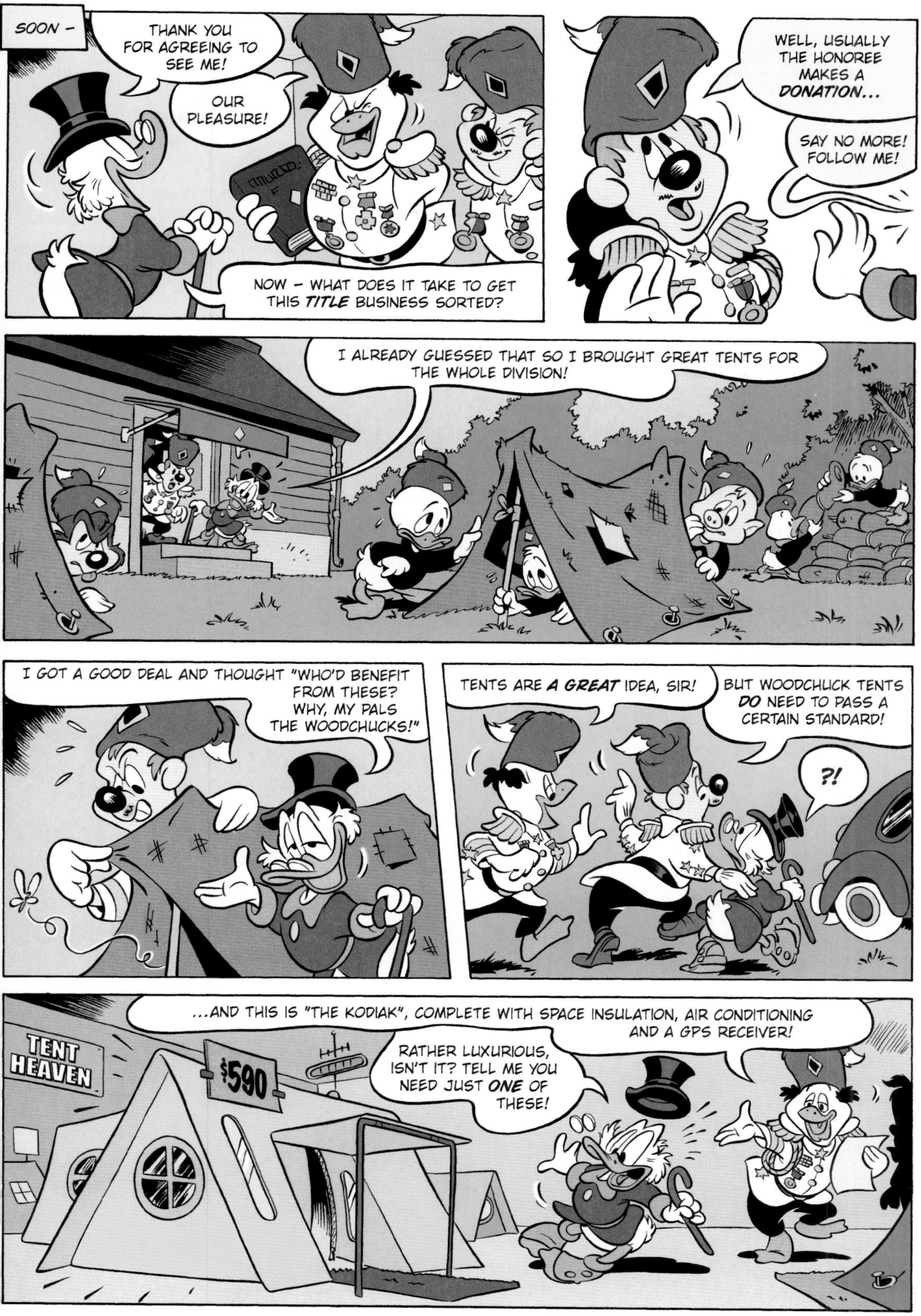
SOON –
THANK YOU FOR AGREEING TO SEE ME!
OUR PLEASURE!
NOW – WHAT DOES IT TAKE TO GET THIS TITLE BUSINESS SORTED?
WELL, USUALLY THE HONOREE MAKES A DONATION...
SAY NO MORE! FOLLOW ME!
I ALREADY GUESSED THAT SO I BROUGHT GREAT TENTS FOR THE WHOLE DIVISION!
I GOT A GOOD DEAL AND THOUGHT "WHO'D BENEFIT FROM THESE? WHY, MY PALS THE WOODCHUCKS!"
TENTS ARE A GREAT IDEA, SIR!
BUT WOODCHUCK TENTS DO NEED TO PASS A CERTAIN STANDARD!
?!
TENT HEAVEN
$590
...AND THIS IS "THE KODIAK", COMPLETE WITH SPACE INSULATION, AIR CONDITIONING AND A GPS RECEIVER!
RATHER LUXURIOUS, ISN'T IT? TELL ME YOU NEED JUST ONE OF THESE!

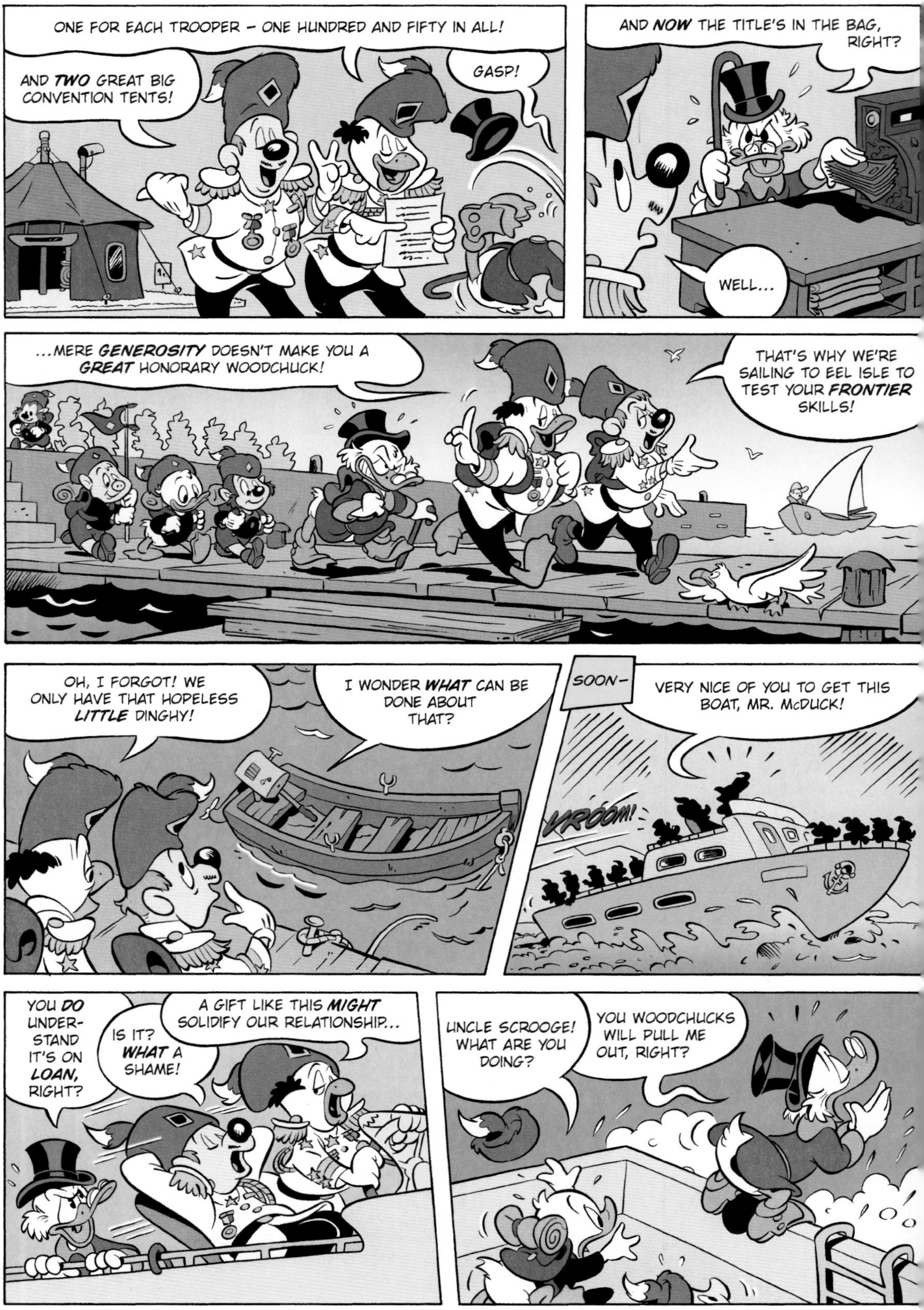
ONE FOR EACH TROOPER – ONE HUNDRED AND FIFTY IN ALL!
AND TWO GREAT BIG CONVENTION TENTS!
GASP!
AND NOW THE TITLE'S IN THE BAG, RIGHT?
WELL...
...MERE GENEROSITY DOESN'T MAKE YOU A GREAT HONORARY WOODCHUCK!
THAT'S WHY WE'RE SAILING TO EEL ISLE TO TEST YOUR FRONTIER SKILLS!
OH, I FORGOT! WE ONLY HAVE THAT HOPELESS LITTLE DINGHY!
I WONDER WHAT CAN BE DONE ABOUT THAT?
SOON–
VERY NICE OF YOU TO GET THIS BOAT, MR. McDUCK!
VROOM!
YOU DO UNDERSTAND IT'S ON LOAN, RIGHT?
IS IT? WHAT A SHAME!
A GIFT LIKE THIS MIGHT SOLIDIFY OUR RELATIONSHIP...
UNCLE SCROOGE! WHAT ARE YOU DOING?
YOU WOODCHUCKS WILL PULL ME OUT, RIGHT?

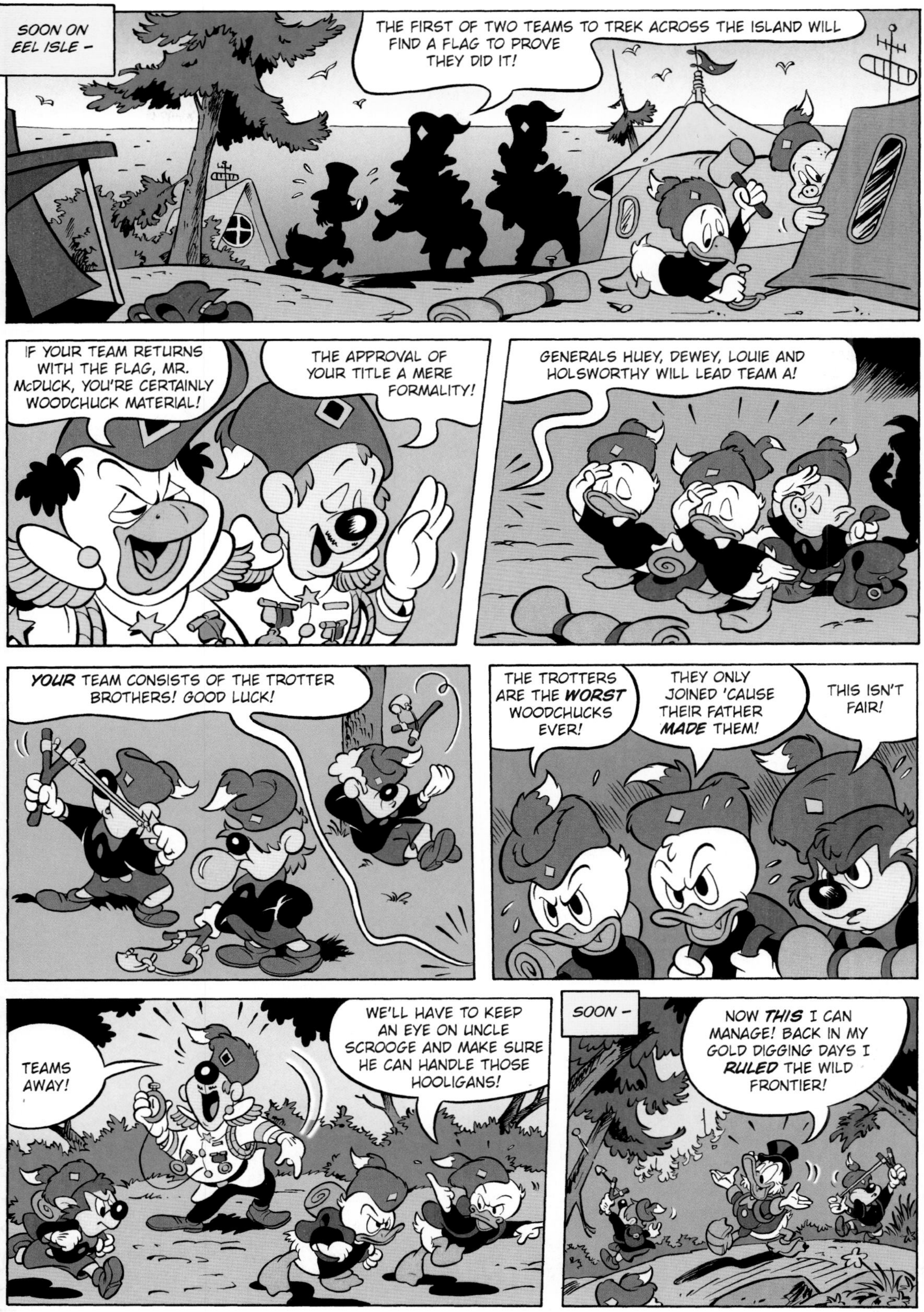
SOON ON EEL ISLE –
THE FIRST OF TWO TEAMS TO TREK ACROSS THE ISLAND WILL FIND A FLAG TO PROVE THEY DID IT!
IF YOUR TEAM RETURNS WITH THE FLAG, MR. McDUCK, YOU'RE CERTAINLY WOODCHUCK MATERIAL!
THE APPROVAL OF YOUR TITLE A MERE FORMALITY!
GENERALS HUEY, DEWEY, LOUIE AND HOLSWORTHY WILL LEAD TEAM A!
YOUR TEAM CONSISTS OF THE TROTTER BROTHERS! GOOD LUCK!
THE TROTTERS ARE THE WORST WOODCHUCKS EVER!
THEY ONLY JOINED 'CAUSE THEIR FATHER MADE THEM!
THIS ISN'T FAIR!
TEAMS AWAY!
WE'LL HAVE TO KEEP AN EYE ON UNCLE SCROOGE AND MAKE SURE HE CAN HANDLE THOSE HOOLIGANS!
SOON –
NOW THIS I CAN MANAGE! BACK IN MY GOLD DIGGING DAYS I RULED THE WILD FRONTIER!

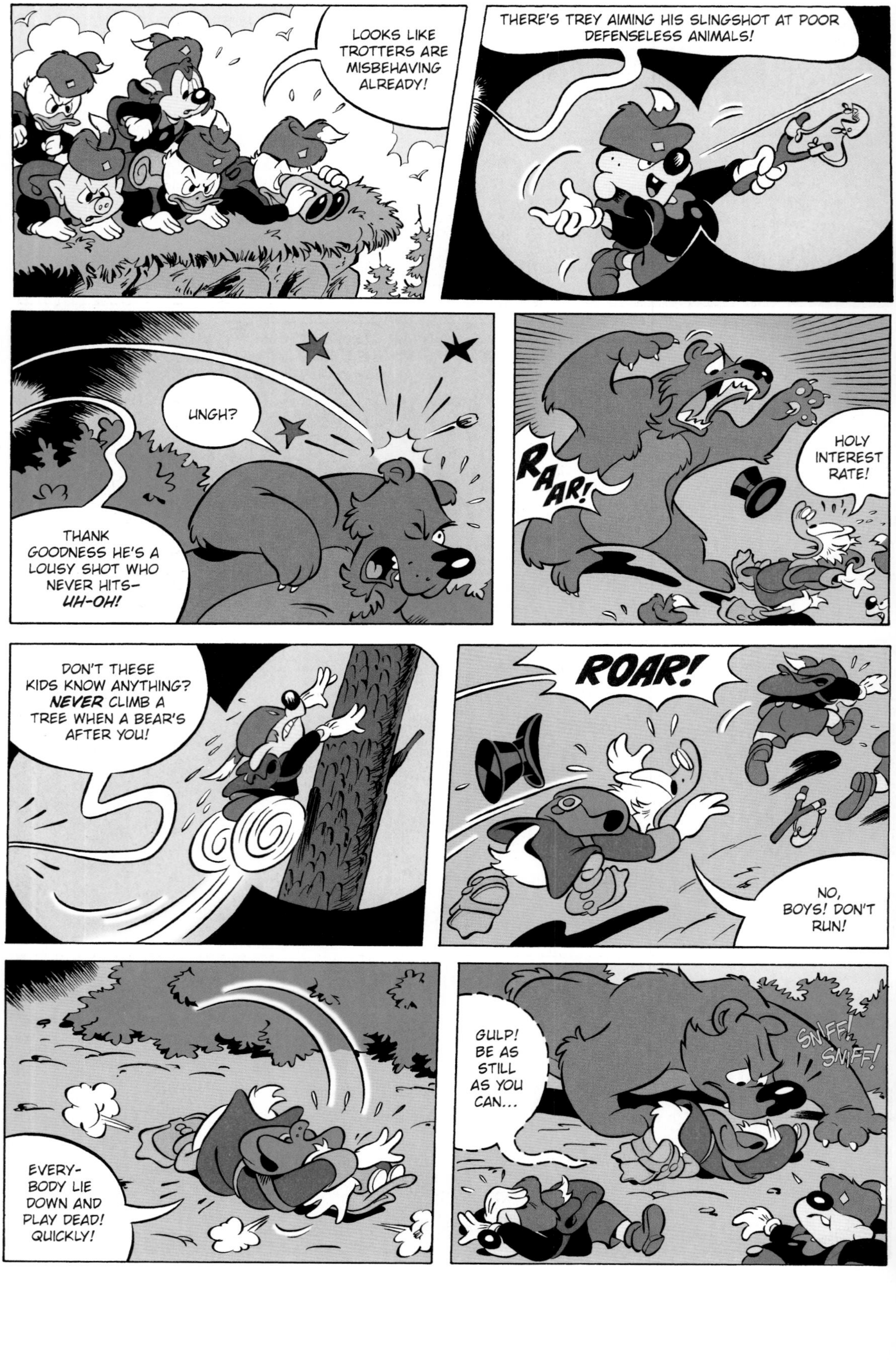
LOOKS LIKE TROTTERS ARE MISBEHAVING ALREADY!
THERE'S TREY AIMING HIS SLINGSHOT AT POOR DEFENSELESS ANIMALS!
UNGH?
THANK GOODNESS HE'S A LOUSY SHOT WHO NEVER HITS— ***UH-OH!***
RAAAR!
HOLY INTEREST RATE!
DON'T THESE KIDS KNOW ANYTHING? ***NEVER*** CLIMB A TREE WHEN A BEAR'S AFTER YOU!
ROAR!
NO, BOYS! DON'T RUN!
EVERY-BODY LIE DOWN AND PLAY DEAD! QUICKLY!
GULP! BE AS STILL AS YOU CAN...
SNIFF! SNIFF!

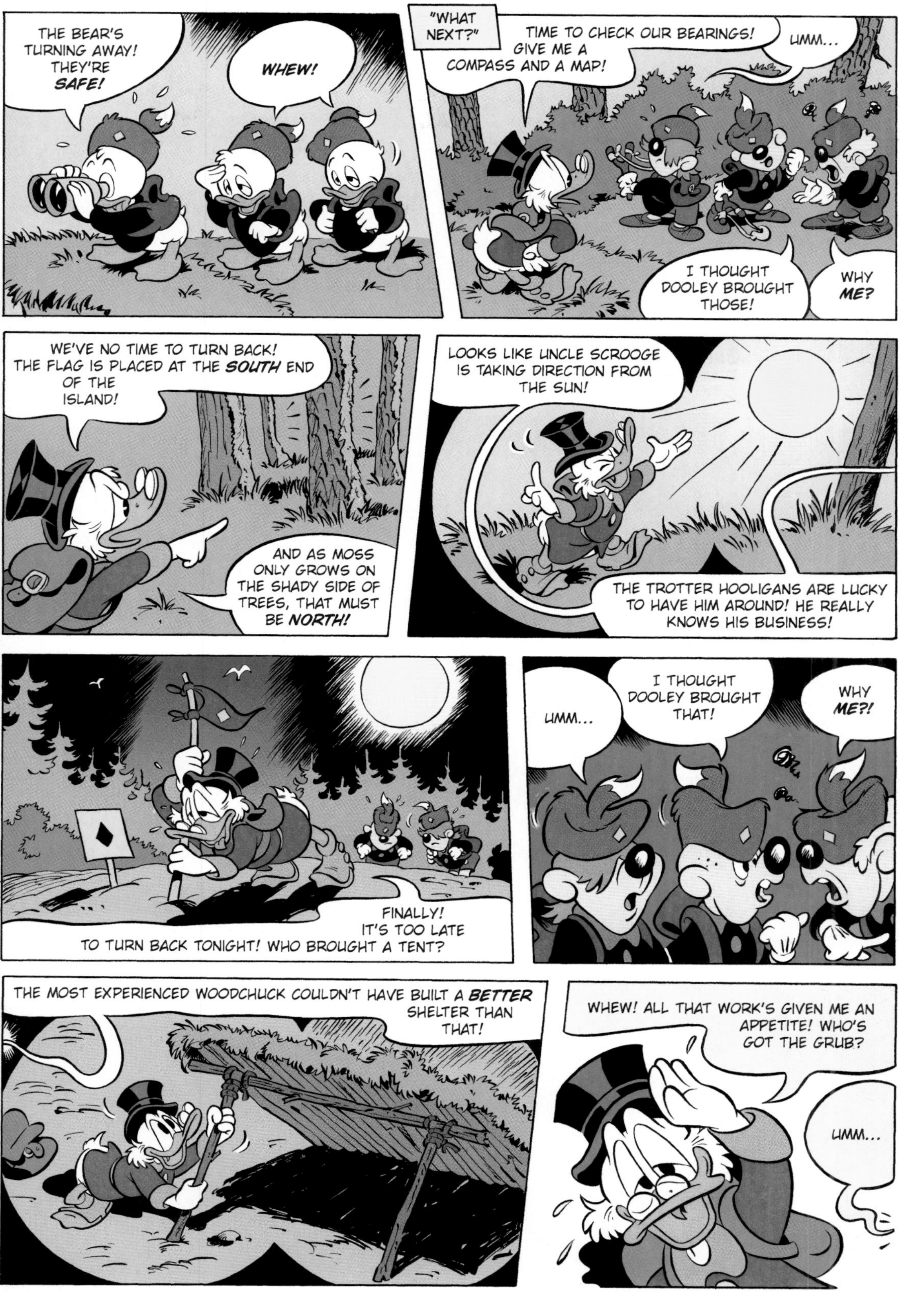
THE BEAR'S TURNING AWAY! THEY'RE SAFE!
WHEW!
"WHAT NEXT?"
TIME TO CHECK OUR BEARINGS! GIVE ME A COMPASS AND A MAP!
UMM...
I THOUGHT DOOLEY BROUGHT THOSE!
WHY ME?
WE'VE NO TIME TO TURN BACK! THE FLAG IS PLACED AT THE SOUTH END OF THE ISLAND!
AND AS MOSS ONLY GROWS ON THE SHADY SIDE OF TREES, THAT MUST BE NORTH!
LOOKS LIKE UNCLE SCROOGE IS TAKING DIRECTION FROM THE SUN!
THE TROTTER HOOLIGANS ARE LUCKY TO HAVE HIM AROUND! HE REALLY KNOWS HIS BUSINESS!
FINALLY! IT'S TOO LATE TO TURN BACK TONIGHT! WHO BROUGHT A TENT?
UMM...
I THOUGHT DOOLEY BROUGHT THAT!
WHY ME?!
THE MOST EXPERIENCED WOODCHUCK COULDN'T HAVE BUILT A BETTER SHELTER THAN THAT!
WHEW! ALL THAT WORK'S GIVEN ME AN APPETITE! WHO'S GOT THE GRUB?
UMM...

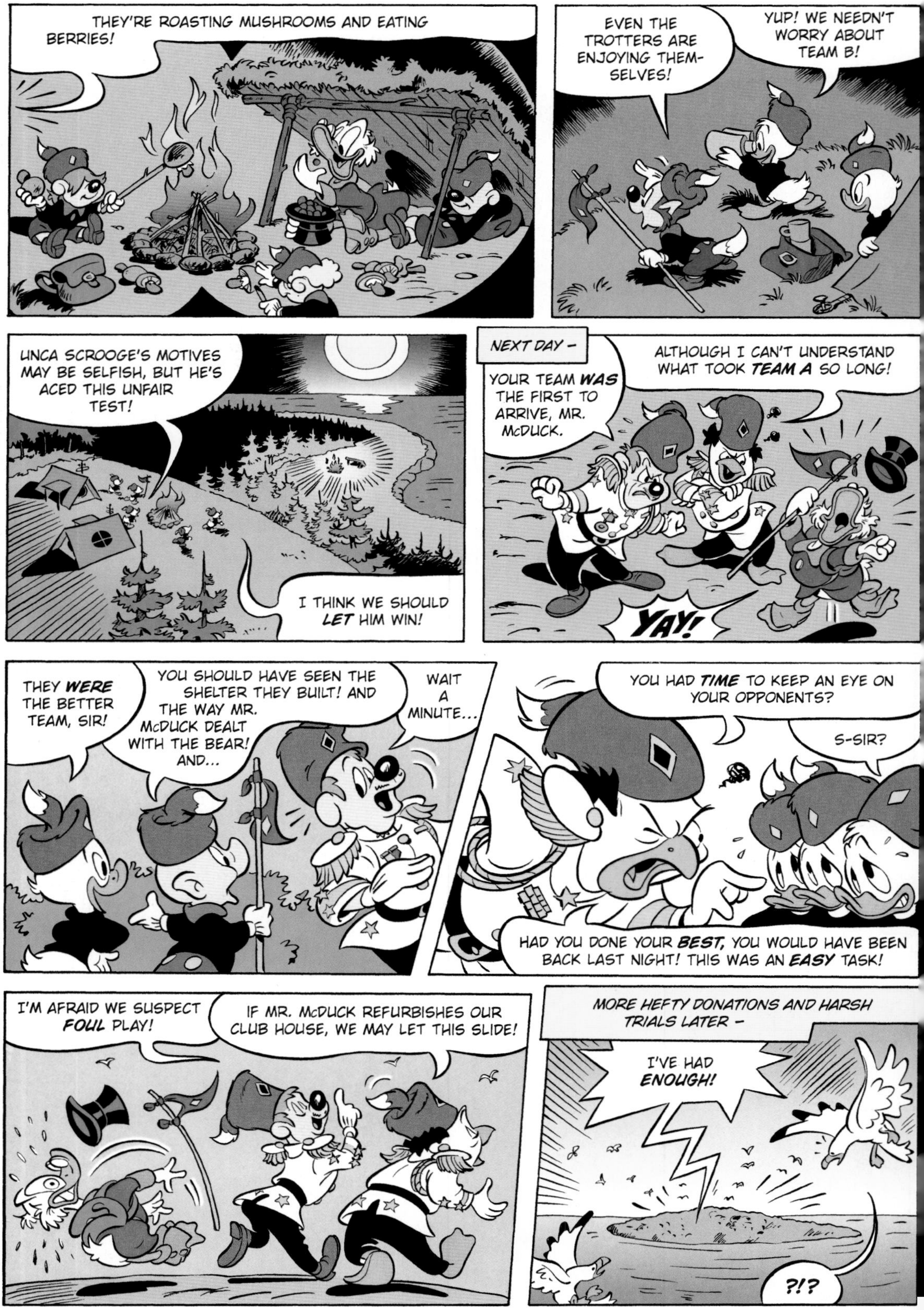
THEY'RE ROASTING MUSHROOMS AND EATING BERRIES!
EVEN THE TROTTERS ARE ENJOYING THEM-SELVES!
YUP! WE NEEDN'T WORRY ABOUT TEAM B!
UNCA SCROOGE'S MOTIVES MAY BE SELFISH, BUT HE'S ACED THIS UNFAIR TEST!
I THINK WE SHOULD LET HIM WIN!
NEXT DAY –
YOUR TEAM WAS THE FIRST TO ARRIVE, MR. McDUCK.
ALTHOUGH I CAN'T UNDERSTAND WHAT TOOK TEAM A SO LONG!
YAY!
THEY WERE THE BETTER TEAM, SIR!
YOU SHOULD HAVE SEEN THE SHELTER THEY BUILT! AND THE WAY MR. McDUCK DEALT WITH THE BEAR! AND...
WAIT A MINUTE...
YOU HAD TIME TO KEEP AN EYE ON YOUR OPPONENTS?
S-SIR?
HAD YOU DONE YOUR BEST, YOU WOULD HAVE BEEN BACK LAST NIGHT! THIS WAS AN EASY TASK!
I'M AFRAID WE SUSPECT FOUL PLAY!
IF MR. McDUCK REFURBISHES OUR CLUB HOUSE, WE MAY LET THIS SLIDE!
MORE HEFTY DONATIONS AND HARSH TRIALS LATER –
I'VE HAD ENOUGH!
?!?

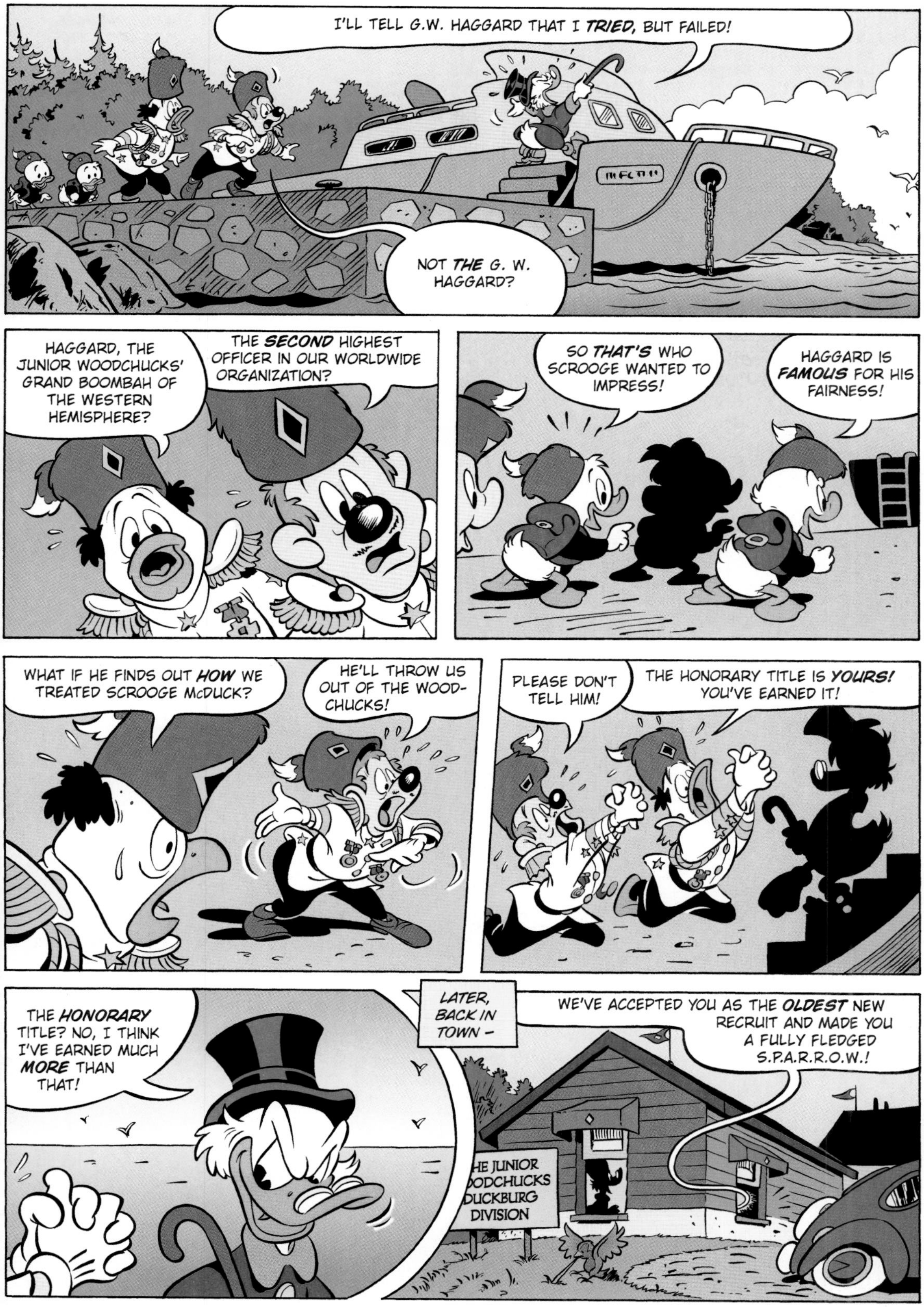
I'LL TELL G.W. HAGGARD THAT I TRIED, BUT FAILED!
NOT THE G. W. HAGGARD?
HAGGARD, THE JUNIOR WOODCHUCKS' GRAND BOOMBAH OF THE WESTERN HEMISPHERE?
THE SECOND HIGHEST OFFICER IN OUR WORLDWIDE ORGANIZATION?
SO THAT'S WHO SCROOGE WANTED TO IMPRESS!
HAGGARD IS FAMOUS FOR HIS FAIRNESS!
WHAT IF HE FINDS OUT HOW WE TREATED SCROOGE McDUCK?
HE'LL THROW US OUT OF THE WOOD-CHUCKS!
PLEASE DON'T TELL HIM!
THE HONORARY TITLE IS YOURS! YOU'VE EARNED IT!
THE HONORARY TITLE? NO, I THINK I'VE EARNED MUCH MORE THAN THAT!
LATER, BACK IN TOWN -
WE'VE ACCEPTED YOU AS THE OLDEST NEW RECRUIT AND MADE YOU A FULLY FLEDGED S.P.A.R.R.O.W.!
HE JUNIOR
OODCHUCKS
UCKBURG
DIVISION

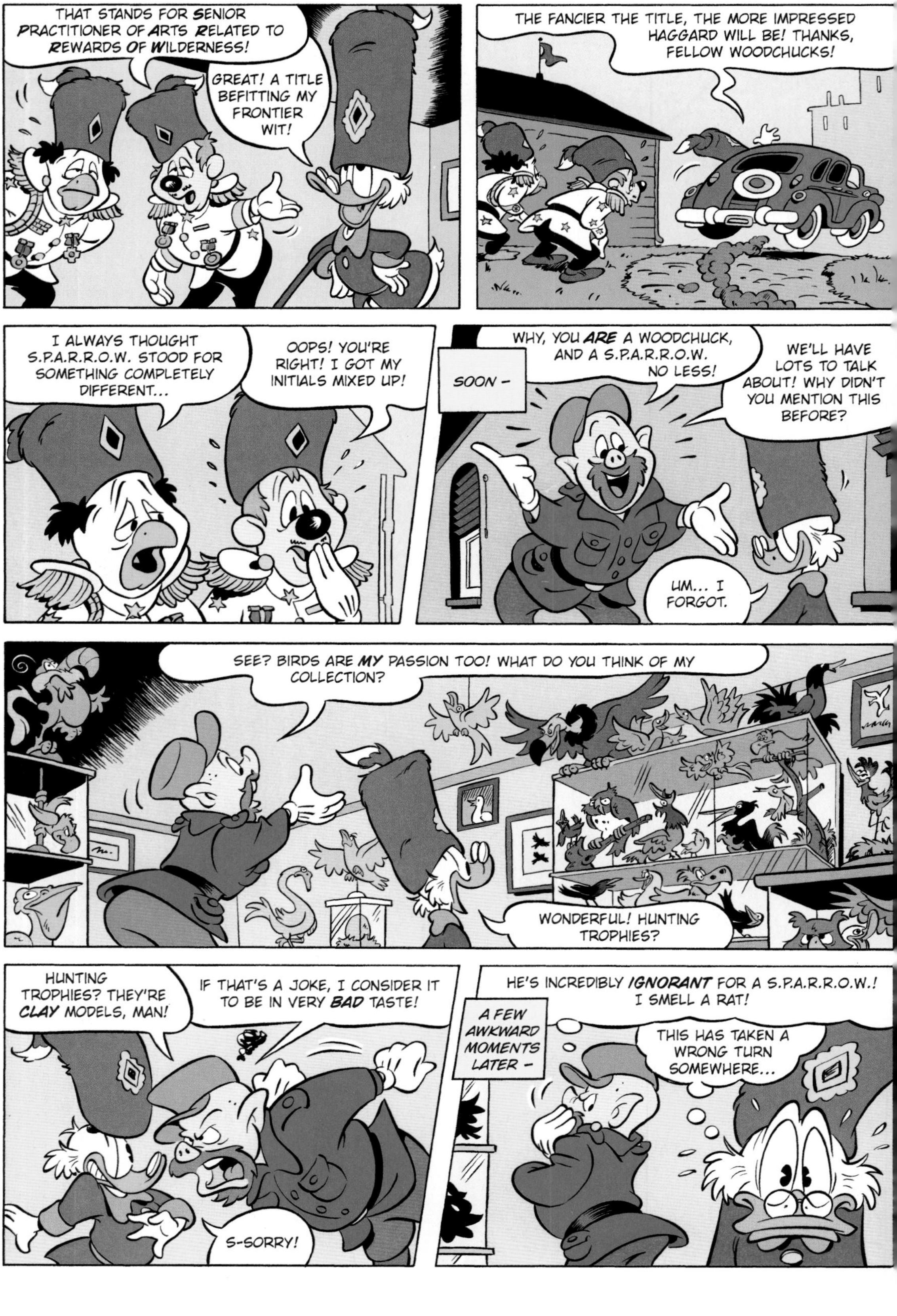
THAT STANDS FOR SENIOR PRACTITIONER OF ARTS RELATED TO REWARDS OF WILDERNESS!
GREAT! A TITLE BEFITTING MY FRONTIER WIT!
THE FANCIER THE TITLE, THE MORE IMPRESSED HAGGARD WILL BE! THANKS, FELLOW WOODCHUCKS!
I ALWAYS THOUGHT S.P.A.R.R.O.W. STOOD FOR SOMETHING COMPLETELY DIFFERENT...
OOPS! YOU'RE RIGHT! I GOT MY INITIALS MIXED UP!
SOON –
WHY, YOU ARE A WOODCHUCK, AND A S.P.A.R.R.O.W. NO LESS!
WE'LL HAVE LOTS TO TALK ABOUT! WHY DIDN'T YOU MENTION THIS BEFORE?
UM... I FORGOT.
SEE? BIRDS ARE MY PASSION TOO! WHAT DO YOU THINK OF MY COLLECTION?
WONDERFUL! HUNTING TROPHIES?
HUNTING TROPHIES? THEY'RE CLAY MODELS, MAN!
IF THAT'S A JOKE, I CONSIDER IT TO BE IN VERY BAD TASTE!
S-SORRY!
A FEW AWKWARD MOMENTS LATER –
HE'S INCREDIBLY IGNORANT FOR A S.P.A.R.R.O.W.! I SMELL A RAT!
THIS HAS TAKEN A WRONG TURN SOMEWHERE...

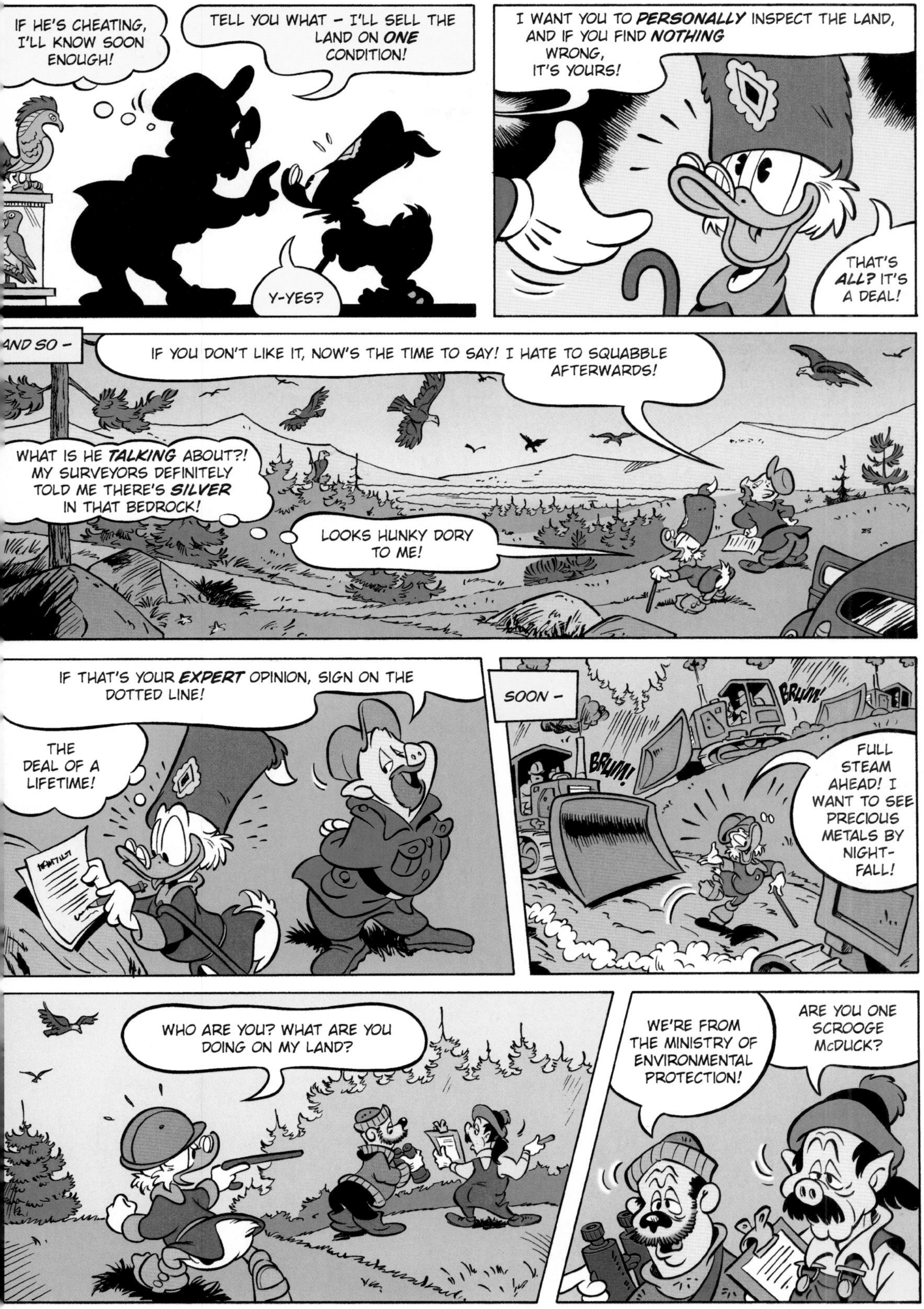
IF HE'S CHEATING, I'LL KNOW SOON ENOUGH!
TELL YOU WHAT – I'LL SELL THE LAND ON ONE CONDITION!
Y-YES?
I WANT YOU TO PERSONALLY INSPECT THE LAND, AND IF YOU FIND NOTHING WRONG, IT'S YOURS!
THAT'S ALL? IT'S A DEAL!
AND SO –
IF YOU DON'T LIKE IT, NOW'S THE TIME TO SAY! I HATE TO SQUABBLE AFTERWARDS!
WHAT IS HE TALKING ABOUT?! MY SURVEYORS DEFINITELY TOLD ME THERE'S SILVER IN THAT BEDROCK!
LOOKS HUNKY DORY TO ME!
IF THAT'S YOUR EXPERT OPINION, SIGN ON THE DOTTED LINE!
THE DEAL OF A LIFETIME!
SOON –
BRUM!
BRUM!
FULL STEAM AHEAD! I WANT TO SEE PRECIOUS METALS BY NIGHT-FALL!
WHO ARE YOU? WHAT ARE YOU DOING ON MY LAND?
WE'RE FROM THE MINISTRY OF ENVIRONMENTAL PROTECTION!
ARE YOU ONE SCROOGE McDUCK?

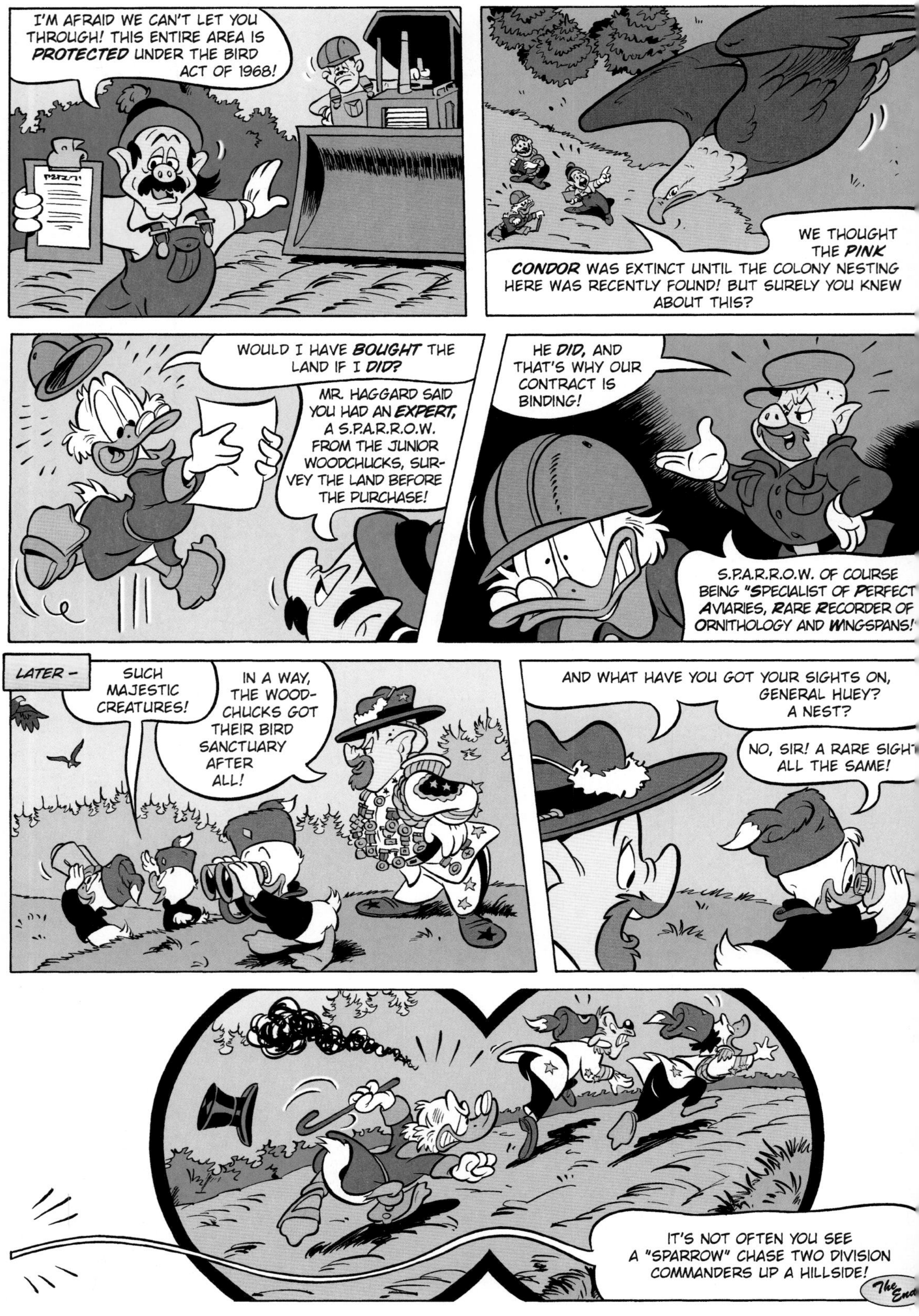
I'M AFRAID WE CAN'T LET YOU THROUGH! THIS ENTIRE AREA IS PROTECTED UNDER THE BIRD ACT OF 1968!
WE THOUGHT THE PINK CONDOR WAS EXTINCT UNTIL THE COLONY NESTING HERE WAS RECENTLY FOUND! BUT SURELY YOU KNEW ABOUT THIS?
WOULD I HAVE BOUGHT THE LAND IF I DID?
MR. HAGGARD SAID YOU HAD AN EXPERT, A S.P.A.R.R.O.W. FROM THE JUNIOR WOODCHUCKS, SURVEY THE LAND BEFORE THE PURCHASE!
HE DID, AND THAT'S WHY OUR CONTRACT IS BINDING!
S.P.A.R.R.O.W. OF COURSE BEING "SPECIALIST OF PERFECT AVIARIES, RARE RECORDER OF ORNITHOLOGY AND WINGSPANS!"
LATER —
SUCH MAJESTIC CREATURES!
IN A WAY, THE WOODCHUCKS GOT THEIR BIRD SANCTUARY AFTER ALL!
AND WHAT HAVE YOU GOT YOUR SIGHTS ON, GENERAL HUEY? A NEST?
NO, SIR! A RARE SIGHT ALL THE SAME!
IT'S NOT OFTEN YOU SEE A "SPARROW" CHASE TWO DIVISION COMMANDERS UP A HILLSIDE!
The End

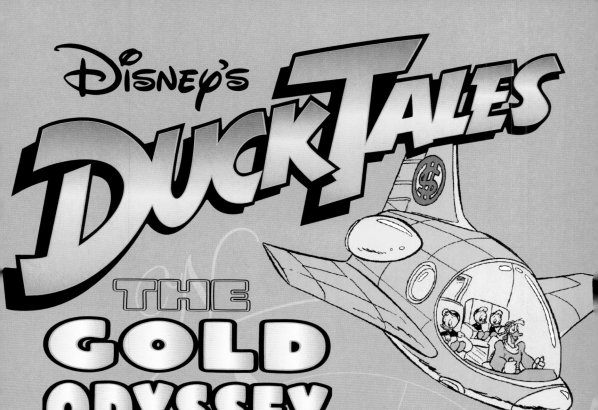
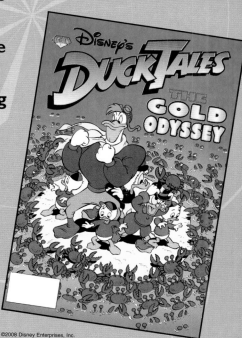

IT'S A JR. WOODCHUCKS

EXTRAVAGANZA!

Illustrations by
DAAN JIPPES

Stories and Inspiration by
CARL BARKS

"The Daan Jippes Collection" is a new trade paperback series collecting the work of this beloved Dutch Duck Man. The first volume features a selection of his "recreations" of Carl Barks tales written but not originally drawn by Barks. Stories include "Duckmade Disaster," with Uncle Scrooge, and "Traitor in the Ranks," costarring Donald Duck. Look for it at your favorite comic book store.

© 2008 Disney Enterprises, Inc.

$8.99

Walt Disney's
DONALD DUCK FAMILY
THE DAAN JIPPES COLLECTION

McDUCK HIGHWAY CONSTRUCTION

www.gemstonepub.com/disney